T0316555

Cambridge Elements

Elements in Music Since 1945
edited by
Mervyn Cooke
University of Nottingham

HERBERT EIMERT AND THE DARMSTADT SCHOOL

The Consolidation of the Avant-Garde

Max Erwin
University of Leeds

CAMBRIDGE
UNIVERSITY PRESS

CAMBRIDGE
UNIVERSITY PRESS

University Printing House, Cambridge CB2 8BS, United Kingdom

One Liberty Plaza, 20th Floor, New York, NY 10006, USA

477 Williamstown Road, Port Melbourne, VIC 3207, Australia

314–321, 3rd Floor, Plot 3, Splendor Forum, Jasola District Centre, New Delhi – 110025, India

79 Anson Road, #06–04/06, Singapore 079906

Cambridge University Press is part of the University of Cambridge.

It furthers the University's mission by disseminating knowledge in the pursuit of education, learning, and research at the highest international levels of excellence.

www.cambridge.org
Information on this title: www.cambridge.org/9781108799713
DOI: 10.1017/9781108891691

First published 2020

A catalogue record for this publication is available from the British Library.

ISBN 978-1-108-79971-3 Paperback
ISSN 2632-7791 (online)
ISSN 2632-7783 (print)

Herbert Eimert and the Darmstadt School

The Consolidation of the Avant-Garde

Elements in Music Since 1945

DOI: 10.1017/9781108891691
First published online: November 2020

Max Erwin
University of Leeds

Author for correspondence: Max Erwin, mc15moe@leeds.ac.uk

Abstract: After 1951, the discourse surrounding both the Darmstadt courses in particular and European New Music more broadly shifted away from a dodecaphonic vocabulary in favour of concepts such as 'punctual music', 'post-Webern music', and 'static music', all collected under the newly christened unity of the Darmstadt School. This study proposes a genealogy of the Darmstadt School through the institutional influence and writings of Herbert Eimert.

It demonstrates that Eimert's understanding of music history – whereby technical procedures are universalised as the acme of historical progress – was adopted as the institutional discourse of New Music in Europe, and remains central to both textbook and critical scholarly accounts which attempt to make sense of the avant-garde after World War II.

Keywords: Darmstadt, serialism, New Music, Webern, institutional studies

ISBNs: 9781108799713 (PB), 9781108891691 (OC)
ISSNs: 2632-7791 (online), 2632-7783 (print)

Contents

1 Introduction

This is not, in any consistent sense, a study of Herbert Eimert's life, times, or music. Nor is it concerned with presenting a particularly detailed reading of his thought and writings about music. In fact, it argues that these writings enunciate a largely unaltered understanding of New Music over the course of almost half a century. Rather, it is expressly concerned with the relatively brief period of time at the beginning of the 1950s when Eimert's understanding of New Music became the institutional discourse of New Music, which, more importantly and more to the point, in turn became the discourse which historians continue to deploy to explicate the development of the musical avant-garde in Europe after World War II – an avant-garde invariantly clustered in discursive formations of 'post-Webern music', 'punctual music', and the 'Darmstadt School'. This study does not propose to account for how or why Eimert devised these concepts, but it does demonstrate definitively that they came from him.

I do not give this demonstration as a sort of conspiratorial revelation; the prominence of cultural gatekeepers in the professional development of young composers is surely not a new and unexpected subject for scholarship. What is new and unexpected is (1) that Eimert's blueprint for a 'punctual' avant-garde predates the 'punctual' works by Stockhausen by nearly thirty years; (2) that Eimert used the practices of now-obscure composers to explicate the practices of now-prominent ones, rendering explanations of what 'Darmstadt composers' were doing fundamentally confused and skewed; and (3) that this discourse is still deployed to explain New Music in the 1950s. The point here is that the discourse precedes the practice. As such, the explication for these musical practices under the Darmstadt banner – practices which, as a very large quantity of very thorough research has demonstrated, are far from uniform and in fact are quite nearly incommensurable under a single label – only deals with the music itself in a cursory, epiphenomenal manner.[1] Consequently, the practice of music historiography has hitherto not dealt with this music at all. It has only dealt with the discourse Eimert made for it.

---

[1] I am referring specifically to Martin Iddon, *New Music at Darmstadt: Nono, Stockhausen, Cage, and Boulez* (Cambridge: Cambridge University Press, 2013); M. J. Grant, *Serial Music, Serial Aesthetics: Compositional Theory in Post-War Europe* (Cambridge: Cambridge University Press, 2001); Mark Delaere, 'Olivier Messiaen's Analysis Seminar and the Development of Post-War Serial Music', trans. Richard Evans, *Music Analysis*, 21.1 (2002), 35–51; Inge Kovács, *Wege zum musikalischen Strukturalismus: René Leibowitz, Pierre Boulez, John Cage und die Webern-Rezeption in Paris um 1950* (Schliengen: Argus, 2004); Christopher Fox, 'Darmstadt and the Institutionalisation of Modernism', *Contemporary Music Review*, 26.1 (2007), 115–23; Björn Heile, 'Darmstadt as Other: British and American Responses to Musical Modernism', *Twentieth-Century Music*, 1.2 (2004), 161–78; Paul Attinello, 'Postmodern or Modern: A Different Approach to Darmstadt', *Contemporary Music Review*, 26.1 (2007), 25–37, in addition to others cited *passim*.

A certain amount of historical scene-setting is necessary to appreciate Eimert's interventions, and I hope to accomplish it quickly and relatively elegantly with a brief summary of the institution of Darmstadt and its key players from its inception in 1946 until 1951, when Eimert comes to the fore as a distinct cultural force. Karel Goeyvaerts, a Belgian composer who had recently completed his studies in Paris with Olivier Messiaen and Darius Milhaud, arrived at the 1951 courses after a series of early career successes, including a performance at the International Society for Contemporary Music (ISCM) World Music Days of 1950. Goeyvaerts, who had previously incorporated elements of his Roman Catholic faith into his compositions (his *Tre lieder per sonare a venti-sei*, for example, calls for an altar bell, typically rung when the celebrant gives the Eucharistic Prayer), now developed a sophisticated metaphysical method of composition in conjunction with fellow student Jean Barraqué.[2] Both devout Catholics, Barraqué and Goeyvaerts expanded on several compositional techniques of their teacher Messiaen, who himself described his compositional practice as a method of expressing 'the theology and the truths of our Catholic faith'.[3] The result was a series of structural devices – crosses, mirror-symmetries, ciphers based on holy numbers – that largely eliminated the sorts of subjective decision-making that might normally be considered to be part of compositional craft. Indeed, Goeyvaerts termed this new ideal 'selfless music', the end result being a purified sound world that approximated a Neo-Platonic higher divine order removed from human experience. Karlheinz Stockhausen, a composition student four years younger than Goeyvaerts and himself a devout Roman Catholic, encountered Goeyvaerts at the 1951 Darmstädter Ferienkurse and was deeply impressed with the older composer's new method of composition, adopting it himself in *Kreuzspiel*, which he began immediately after the 1951 courses and completed in early 1952, with advice from Goeyvaerts. During the same period, Herbert Eimert was beginning to enlarge his sphere of influence as a cultural gatekeeper at the NWDR (Nordwestdeutscher Rundfunk; later Westdeutscherrundfunk, WDR), and had made the acquaintance of both Goeyvaerts and Stockhausen, taking the latter tightly under his wing.[4] The consequences of this relationship are the

---

[2] See Max Erwin, 'Who Is Buried in Webern's Tomb? Orientations in the Reception of Serial Music from Messiaen to Stockhausen', *Perspectives of New Music,* in press.

[3] Olivier Messiaen, *The Technique of My Musical Language*, trans. John Satterfield (Paris: Alphonse Leduc, 1956), I.13.

[4] Goeyvaerts had met Eimert at the 1950 ISCM New Music Days; Eimert was particularly impressed that Goeyvaerts had a score of Webern's Second Cantata, which had not been published yet, and the two followed this score during the performance of the piece. See Karel Goeyvaerts, 'Paris – Darmstadt: 1947–1956: Excerpt from the Autobiographical Portrait', trans. Mark Delaere, *Revue belge de Musicologie/Belgisch Tijdschrift voor Muziekwetenschap,* 48 (1994), 39. Helmut Kirchmeyer suggests that Eimert's relationship to the young Stockhausen was

focus of this study, and its central purpose is to demonstrate how Eimert deployed the compositional techniques used by Goeyvaerts and Stockhausen as a universal technical programme for New Music. Largely through Eimert's influence, the early practice of Goeyvaerts and Stockhausen became the house style of the Darmstadt School, even though virtually no other composers – and certainly not their prominent peers Luigi Nono, Bruno Maderna, and Pierre Boulez – adopted these techniques or their attendant metaphysical ideology.

On to Darmstadt. At the outset of the 1946 courses, director Wolfgang Steinecke described their objective in negative terms, as a necessary corrective to 'a criminal cultural politics that robbed German musical life of its leading personalities and its connection with the world'.[5] The primary rhetorical objective of the courses at their inception, then, was one of internationalisation and 'catching up' to the outside world (*Nachholbedarf*). It was uncertain, as the press response to the 1947 courses makes clear, whether a coherent avant-garde, let alone a modernist New Music, was to play any part in their proceedings. In retrospect, then, the courses are hardly recognisable as the historical Darmstadt at this stage; Iddon's thorough prehistory describes them as 'ramshackle affairs in most respects', to the extent that they primarily functioned 'as experiments in finding out what the courses could be and how they might function'.[6] Such a confusion of purpose in retrospect problematises the usual historiographical demarcations and conceptual vocabulary deployed to explicate the post-war avant-garde, especially the 'zero hour' myth. Contrary to Steinecke's inaugural address, the first courses extensively programmed the work of composers implicated in the Nazi regime, and numerous works by such composers were heavily represented in the two following iterations.[7] While many of the more compromised of these composers were dropped from the programmes of later

---

close enough to be that of a foster father; see below and Kirchmeyer, *Kleine Monographie über Herbert Eimert* (Leipzig: Sächsischen Akademie der Wissenschaften, 1998), 9.

[5] '[E]ine verbrecherische Kulturpolitik das deutsche Musikleben seiner führenden Persönlichkeiten und seines Zusammenhanges mit der Welt beraubt.' Wolfgang Steinecke, reproduced in Gianmario Borio and Hermann Danuser, eds., *Im Zenit der Moderne: Die Internationalen Ferienkurse für Neue Musik Darmstadt 1946–1966* (Freiburg: Rombach, 1997), I.24–5. All translations by the author unless otherwise noted.

[6] Iddon, *New Music at Darmstadt*, 21. Iddon's subsequent claim that Steinecke was 'guided more by contingency than by ideology' during this period might be nuanced by the suggestion that Steinecke was indeed guided by ideology, just not a very clear or consistent one.

[7] In addition to Carl Orff, Hermann Heiß, and Wolfgang Fortner: Werner Egk, Kurt Hessenberg, Helmut Degen, Ottmar Gerster, Gerhard Frommel, Harald Genzmer, Hugo Distler, Karl Marx, Ernst Pepping, Franz Flößner, Erich Sehlbach, Hugo Herrmann, Gerhard Schwarz, Paul Höffer, Hermann Reutter, Othmar Schoeck, Bruno Stürmer, Wilhelm Maler, and others. It should be noted, however, that such a repertoire was about the norm for programmes of contemporary art music in the aftermath of the war; see Ian Pace, 'The Reconstruction of Post-War West German New Music during the early Allied Occupation (1945–46), and its Roots in the Weimar Republic and Third Reich (1918–45)' (unpublished PhD thesis, University of Cardiff, 2018), appendices.

courses (e.g. Ernst Pepping and Kurt Hessenberg), other compromised figures, like Carl Orff and Wolfgang Fortner, continued to be prominently featured throughout the decade.

From the outset, then, it is essential to maintain that the instrumentality of Darmstadt as discourse cannot be easily reconciled with the majority of the concrete administrative and programmatic decisions that were made about the courses themselves. A historical account solely focused on the latter would be able to present only the most glacial changes of repertoire over the first twenty years of the courses' existence.[8] Discursively, on the other hand, Darmstadt moves in lurches and jolts. The suture of Steinecke's internationalist project to Leibowitz and Adorno's historicist project, initiated in 1948 with the advent of Leibowitz as composition faculty and accomplished in 1950 with Steinecke's announcement that Schoenberg's work and thought formed the 'pedagogical foundation' and 'primary departure point for work within the courses',[9] enacted a categorical re-grounding of the courses, presenting their pedagogical purpose as not only a social (i.e. internationalist) but also an aesthetic one aligned with a singular New Music. For about two years, this suture held in the critical discourse, and press reports, while disparaging, described a singular avant-garde of young composers at the forefront of the courses advancing a coherent and mutually understood aesthetic project, as in Stuckenschmidt's grouping of works by Antoine Duhamel, André Casanova, and Michel Philippot (all current students of Leibowitz) as representing at once 'the most aggressive of twelve-tone technique' and 'the danger of Leibowitzian radicalism'.[10] Borio sums up this period elegantly: 'Between 1948 and 1951, most of the young composers working in Darmstadt adopted twelve-tone technique'.[11]

Of course, in their explicit function as a forum for post-Schoenbergian dodecaphony, the Darmstadt courses operated as host to a musical practice which had been extensively theorised and developed over a vast global network. In rhetoric which might suggest to a cynical mind that the international charter of the courses had never been taken as an article of good faith, Stuckenschmidt repeatedly emphasises how such an alien practice had been artificially imported to Darmstadt by Leibowitz and his school.[12] It is representative that the Second International Twelve-Tone Congress whose proceedings occupied three days of

---

[8]   To be sure, such an enterprise would be a welcome rejoinder to the lingering monumentalism of music historiography; nevertheless, its chronological scope exceeds that of the present study.

[9]   Hermann Danuser, 'Die "Darmstädter Schule" – Faktizität und Mythos', in *Im Zenit der Moderne*, II.341.

[10]   See Stuckenschmidt, 'Apokalyptische Gespräche', in *Im Zenit der Moderne*, III.390.

[11]   'Zwischen 1948 und 1951 eignen sich die meisten in Darmstadt wirkenden jungen Komponisten die Zwölftontechnik an.' Borio, 'Kontinuität der Moderne?', *Im Zenit der Moderne*, I.187.

[12]   Stuckenschmidt, 'Apokalyptische Gespräche', 389.

the 1951 courses was an independently organised and constituted entity to which Darmstadt provided a forum – a forum which had previously been in Milan. At the conclusion of the Milan session, Wladimir Vogel, who co-organised the congress with Malipiero, envisioned an expansion of its peda-gogical scope – a 'more extensive meeting than the Milanese one' with the introduction of 'working groups'.[13] After Vogel's initial plans to organise the next congress in Locarno fell through, Steinecke intervened and proposed the Darmstadt courses as a potential venue.[14] Not only would the congress have a captive audience, its activities would be integrated within the pedagogical apparatus of the courses, with Schoenberg himself leading a composition seminar.[15] Matters did not proceed entirely as planned. Schoenberg soon can-celled due to serious illness (although not soon enough to prevent the advertis-ing of his presence); Steinecke offered leadership of Schoenberg's session to Vogel, who modestly declined and then later demurred from attending the congress altogether.[16] He was, of course, ultimately replaced by Adorno. Carlo Piccardi's study of the Dodecaphonic Congress emplots the moment of Vogel's abdication as the bookend to the dodecaphonic era more broadly, with the young Darmstadt composers at the 1951 courses exclusively engaged with the radical 'post-Webernian current', in effect resulting in 'a second avant-garde'.[17]

Piccardi and Borio's bracketing, once again, is a discursive one. If the 1951 courses may be read as a victory lap or high-water mark of international dode-caphony, such a demarcation is far less visible in the musical practices repre-sented at the courses or the congress itself. To be sure, the congress programme was, on its own terms, a systematic one, moving from a discussion on a 'systematic representation of "classic" twelve-tone technique and its possibil-ities' to the 'possibilities for continuation of twelve-tone technique (mutations of such in the work of younger composers)'.[18] And Goeyvaerts's recollection that the twelve-tone method 'had caught on', like Piccardi and Borio's periodisation,

---

[13] Carlo Piccardi, 'Tra ragioni umane e ragioni estetiche: i dodecafonici a congresso', in *Norme con Ironie: scritti per i settant'anni di Ennio Morricone*, ed. Laura Gallenga (Milan: Suivini Zerboni, 1998), 250.

[14] Steinecke to Vogel, 21 November 1950; cited in Piccardi, 'Tra ragioni', 250.   [15] Ibid.

[16] See Piccardi, 'Tra ragioni', 251. Piccardi characterises Vogel's excuses as 'trivial', but astutely concludes that the composer was probably far more comfortable remaining in Switzerland (it is not difficult to imagine Vogel seeing the transition from lakeside Locarno to Woog-side Darmstadt as a considerable downgrade, institutional apparatus notwithstanding).

[17] Ibid.

[18] 'Systematische Darstellung der "klassischen" Zwölftontechnik und ihrer Möglichkeiten', 'Erweiterungsmöglichkeiten der Zwölftontechnik (Mutationen derselbe im Schaffen der jüngeren Komponisten)'; occurring on 3 July and 4 July 1951, respectively. See *Im Zenit der Moderne*, III.548.

is partially borne out by the programmed concerts, which featured the more reliable of the younger dodecaphonists like Henze, Togni, and Wildberger.[19] But such a discursive stability was negotiated against musical practices which were far less stable and systematic: Wildberger's piece, for example, was immediately followed by Goeyvaerts's in the second 'Musik der jungen Generation' concert.[20] Even the official concert of the congress contained two pieces by Hauer alongside the freely atonal and expressionistic *Zwei Stücke* for clarinet and piano by Egon Wellesz, a composer who Adorno had marked as pursuing a 'bad modernism', with the likes of Werner Egk and Hermann Reutter, which must be resisted.[21] Indeed, the other two representatives of this 'bad modernism' had been programmed, alongside Carl Orff, on the opening concert of the 1951 courses.[22] Yet the Second International Twelve-Tone Congress appears from press responses to have been the defining fixture of the courses, with the premiere of Schoenberg's 'Der Tanz um das goldene Kalb' representing its ultimate triumph. Indeed, the ecumenical and stabilising movement of international dodecaphony – Piccardi notes the 'pluralistic' character of the concert programming for the congress in Milan –[23] very nearly appears to have encompassed the entirety of Darmstadt's discursive economy, incorporating even erstwhile dissidents like Hermann Heiß and Herbert Eimert into its service.[24]

There was, nonetheless, a limit to the stability of this discourse, a point past which something of Piccardi's 'second avant-garde' begins to appear. As Schoenberg's replacement, Adorno's composition seminar was the pedagogical extension of the Second International Twelve-Tone Congress. His encounter with Goeyvaerts and Stockhausen, and the minor press attention it generated, runs contrary to the otherwise unqualified focus on dodecaphony as international New Music practice. Adorno's defensive response – the cultic, excentric relegation to *Adrian Leverkühn und sein Famulus* – might well have been the last word if discursive provisions had not been made to integrate the music of the Sonata for Two Pianos into the mainstream of international-institutional New Music.

It is only at this point after the encounter that Webern finally arrives, acting as a retroactive tether to Goeyvaerts and Stockhausen's ex-centric, eccentric, and

---

[19] Ibid., III.547–51.   [20] Ibid., III.550.

[21] Referenced in Gianmario Borio, 'Dire cela, sans savoir quoi: The Question of Meaning in Adorno and in the Musical Avant-Garde', trans. Robert L. Kendrick, in *Apparitions: New Perspectives on Adorno and Twentieth-Century Music*, ed. Berthold Hoeckner (New York: Routledge, 2006), 43.

[22] *Im Zenit der Moderne*, III.544. Egk's offering, an Orchester-Sonate for large orchestra (1948), had previously been performed in the closing concert of the 1948 courses under the composer's baton.

[23] Piccardi, 'Tra ragioni', 228.   [24] *Im Zenit der Moderne*, III.548.

pre-Scholastic practice. Eimert's deployment of Webern, then, operates as a gesture of affirmation – Adorno's orientation, and that of international dodecaphony, is not wrong, Eimert says; it is simply technically insufficient, it has missed the most important, most historically propositional aspects of the very practice it advocates. Eimert accepts international, historically conditioned dodecaphony and its universal validity – most obviously in his role as a participant in the Second International Twelve-Tone Congress, at which he gave a presentation arguing that twelve-tone music is a universal *technique* rather than a mannerist *style* – but proposes a subsequent stage in this historical evolution: 'punctual' music developed from Anton Webern's mature works. [25] Next to Goeyvaerts's and Stockhausen's firm denial of Adorno's practice as a search for chickens in abstract paintings, Eimert here enacts both a reconciliation and an elevation of Adornian-Leibowitzian dodecaphony. Simultaneously, Goeyvaerts's Sonata and Stockhausen's *Kreuzspiel* are not at all aberrations which subsist outside of the teleology of New Music, as Adorno had mistakenly taken them to be. Goeyvaerts and Stockhausen's rejoinder to Adorno, then, becomes just that – an event of course-correction or aesthetic clinamen rather than ideological overhaul. Through the advent of 'punctual music', Adornian-Leibowitzian historicism is not discarded, but enlarged. The discourse of New Music is re-stabilised.

2 After Dodecaphony: Darmstadt 1951

Eimert's institutional clout at the Darmstädter Ferienkurse in 1951 was such that he presented a joint lecture with the director of the courses, Wolfgang Steinecke, titled portentously 'Is Music at an End? An Optimistic Meditation on Musical Limit-Situations'.[26] The lecture is revealing to the extent that it provides a context and a theoretical precedent for the aesthetic-historical positions Eimert would later use to foreground the young Darmstadt composers (although it is unclear to what extent Steinecke also contributed to this lecture). Eimert, in evidently Adornian fashion, positions the New Music as an 'optimistic' opposition to the 'pessimistic' narrative of 'the last Romantics', exemplified in Pfitzner, as well as to the 'turn to a classical austerity' found in Stravinsky,

---

[25] Eimert, 'Zwölftonstil oder Zwölftontechnik?', given 2 July 1951 as the opening talk of the congress; see *Im Zenit der Moderne*, III.548.

[26] 'Ist die Musik am Ende? Eine optimistische Betrachtung über musikalische Grenzsituationen', in *Im Zenit der Moderne: Die Internationalen Ferienkurse für Neue Musik Darmstadt 1946–1966,* ed. Gianmario Borio and Hermann Danuser (Freiburg: Rombach, 1997), III.340–53. The key word *Grenzsituation* hints at the philosophical debt this lecture owes to the work of philosopher Karl Jaspers. Elsewhere, Borio gives the date of this lecture as 1950, but this is surely a *lapsus calami*, since the lecture contains a recording of Nono's *Variazioni canoniche sulla serie dell'op. 41 di Arnold Schoenberg* (1950) which was first performed at the conclusion of the 1950 courses (ibid., I.269).

Bartók, Hindemith, and Honegger.[27] Later, in Steinecke's words, the New Music is characterised – again using terms taken from Karl Jaspers – by *Verbindlichkeit*, which is defined as both 'objective legitimacy of expression and authenticity of form'.[28] Eimert, switching to a polemical mode, then tells his listeners: 'You are now going to hear a series of examples, which represent such typical limit-situations in modern music. It is very extraordinary and extreme musical examples which we bring, they have no "reconciliation" and whoever has based his musical position purely on history, presumably without any inkling of our own historical catastrophe, will hear such music only with the gravest chagrin.'[29]

Strikingly, the examples curated by Eimert are immediately recognisable as something nearly approximating the canonic litany of the European avant-garde that one finds to this day in historical overviews: two pieces, *Intégrales* (1925) and *Ionisation* (1933), by Varèse; *Tre lieder per sonare a venti-sei* by Goeyvaerts; *Le soleil des eaux* by Boulez; *Variazioni canoniche sulla serie dell'op. 41 di Arnold Schoenberg* (1950) by Nono; *Psyché* (1946) by Jolivet (the only example that might look out of place in a textbook New Music canon); and, crucially, Webern's Piano Variations, op. 27 (1936). It is essential to note that, while Varèse and Nono had previously attended the courses, all of the other music deployed by Eimert had, at best, a tenuous relationship to the institution of Darmstadt as it existed in 1951. While Webern's Piano Variations were performed at the 1948 courses, the decision to use such a piece as a foundational criterion of New Music – especially Darmstadtian New Music – was a far from obvious one, since this performance was the only piece of Webern programmed in 1948, in contrast with four pieces by Schoenberg, three each by Bartók, Blacher, Milhaud, and Honegger, and ten by Hindemith (eleven if one counts the new version of *Das Marienleben* (1936–1948), performed in addition to the 1922–1923 version).[30] As such, Eimert here presents for the first time a template for the Darmstadt School: Boulez, Goeyvaerts, and Nono, with Varèse and Webern as their spiritual predecessors. Eimert's curation in effect synthesises a foundation myth for Darmstadt modernism predicated on the operative historicism used by Theodor Adorno and René Leibowitz to establish Schoenbergian dodecaphony as the

---

[27] Ibid., III.341–2. Although Steinecke, perhaps playing the good cop, has some kind words for *Palestrina* (1917).

[28] Ibid., III.343.

[29] 'Sie werden gleich eine Reihe von Beispielen hören, die solche typischen Grenzsituationen der modernen Musik darstellen. Es sind musikalisch außerordentlich extreme Beispiele, die wir bringen, sie haben nichts "Versöhnliches", und wer seine musikalische Position ausschließlich in der Geschichte bezogen hat, vermutlich ohne jegliche Ahnung von unserem eigenen geschichtlichen Verhängnis, der wird solche musik nur mit äußerstem Missvergnügen hören.' Ibid., III.344.

[30] See *Im Zenit der Moderne*, III.527–32.

singular manifestation of historically advanced musical production,[31] a myth whose development was overseen by Eimert himself over the course of the following decade.

Eimert's reading of New Music – since this talk is being given alongside the director of the Ferienkurse, this is undoubtedly institutional, 'official' New Music – inevitably reveals his preoccupation with his own historical status as a composer in post-war Germany. To this end, Varèse's *Ionisation* is seen as a representation of modern warfare, and Eimert criticises the 'ill-adjusted audience' who, oblivious to this, had greeted its performance the previous year in Darmstadt with jeers.[32] Eimert's reading of Webern is still more iconoclastic. Drawing on Thomas Mann's *Doktor Faustus*, Eimert presents Webern's work as a 'taking-back' (*Zurücknahme*) of nineteenth-century romanticism, in parallel with the Faustian composer Adrian Leverkühn's desire to retract the finale of Beethoven's Ninth Symphony.[33] This retraction is at once metaphorical and literal: Eimert uses the conclusion of Leverkühn's (fictional) cantata, where a high cello note is slowly and extremely quietly sustained before finally being overcome by silence, as a thematic analogy to Webern's music, which 'consists of naked row-skeletons and avoids all historical forms (such as fugue, canon, imitation, complementary rhythms, etc.). Anton Webern', he concludes, 'is a master of these history-less and abstract sound-forms, he has, so to speak, conceived – far beyond Schoenberg – twelve-tone music to its end.'[34] Furthermore, Eimert and Steinecke emphasise the hermetic quality of this music, the latter pointing out that, despite its small audience, Webern's music is 'more real' than '*Unterhaltungsmusik*, which inundates humanity like lukewarm bathwater', and the film and radio music heard by millions.[35] As with Varèse, Webern's supposed inaccessibility to a wide public is positioned by Eimert and Steinecke as a crucial legitimising facet of his music.

On the other hand, the younger generation are portrayed as stuck in a creative crisis, unsure of what should come after the Neoclassicism of Stravinsky and Hindemith (which recalls Eimert's rejection of Stockhausen's Drei Lieder as

---

[31] See Theodor Adorno, *Philosophie der neuen Musik*, in *Gesammelte Schriften XII*, ed. Rolf Tiedemann (Frankfurt am Main: Suhrkamp, 1975) and René Leibowitz, *Schoenberg and His School*, trans. Dika Newlin (New York: Philosophical Library, 1949).

[32] Ibid., III.347–8. The trope of the misunderstood composer besieged by an ignorant public, most probably Eimert's personal exegesis of Schoenberg–Adorno's thought, would of course become a cliché of historical narratives of the post-war musical avant-garde.

[33] Ibid., III.348.

[34] ' ... aus nackten Reihengerüsten bestehen und allen historischen Formen (wie Fuge, Kanon, Imitation, komplementäre Rhythmik usw.) bewußt aus dem Wege gehen. Anton Webern ist ein Meister dieser geschichtslos-abstrakten Klangformen, er hat – weit über Schoenberg hinaus – die Zwölftonmusik gewissermaßen zu Ende gedacht.' Ibid., III.348–9.

[35] Ibid., III.349.

'too conservative').[36] Three tentative paths forward are represented by Boulez, Goeyvaerts, and Nono. In Eimert and Steinecke's reckoning, Boulez represents a sort of synthesis between Webern and Schoenberg in his vocal writing, while his use of timbre and rhythm are characteristic of 'young French music' under the influence of Olivier Messiaen.[37] To further illustrate this influence, Eimert and Steinecke play a recording of Goeyvaerts's *Tre lieder per sonare a venti-sei*.[38] Like Boulez, Goeyvaerts is presented as a member of the 'young French school' interested in the 'previously unknown possibilities of sound production', which Steinecke connects back to Varèse.[39] Revealingly, Goeyvaerts's piece is here *contrasted* with the 'strict twelve-tone work' of Nono, with the suggestion that a synthesis between the two is the next necessary historical evolution in New Music: Goeyvaerts's (and Varèse's) timbral innovations lack a strong formal basis and Nono's 'completely new style' is hindered by his 'outdated orchestration'.[40] Eimert and Steinecke's blueprint laid out in this lecture would largely proceed as planned over the next decade at Kranichstein, with some reshuffling of the parts: Goeyvaerts would take Nono's place as the 'strict' serialist and Nono would be presented as representing the sensitive, humanist dimension of the New Music. The synthesis Eimert and Steinecke describe was to be carried out by the composer who became metonymic with the Darmstädter Ferienkurse: Karlheinz Stockhausen.

3 Darmstadt 1952

3.1 Preparations

After Stockhausen's extraordinarily inspiring meeting with Goeyvaerts at the 1951 courses, which culminated in the two young composers performing the second movement of Goeyvaerts's Sonata for Two Pianos (1950–1951) for a bewildered Adorno, Stockhausen immediately started work on a new piece using radically new techniques, first called *Mosiake*, but later, on Goeyvaerts's suggestion, changed to *Kreuzspiel*.[41] He also moved to Paris at the beginning of 1952 in order to study with Messiaen and Milhaud, again inspired by Goeyvaerts's example. Stockhausen's presence in Paris also made him an

---

[36] Ibid., III.350.   [37] Ibid., III.351.

[38] According to Borio and Danhauser, the portion of the lecture which names the piece by Goeyvaerts being played is missing, but from the context (e.g. the mention of the ondes martenot) it can be confidently asserted that the recording played is of the *Tre lieder*. See ibid., III.352.

[39] Ibid., III.352.   [40] Ibid.

[41] See Herman Sabbe, 'Die Einheit der Stockhausen-Zeit: Neue Erkenntnismöglichkeit der seriellen Entwicklung anhand des frühen Wirkens von Stockhausen und Goeyvaerts. Dargestellt aufgrund der Briefe Stockhausens an Goeyvaerts', in *Karlheinz Stockhausen: ... wie die Zeit verging ...*, Musik-Konzepte, 19 (Munich: text + kritik, 1981), 18.

essential liaison for the Darmstadt courses, through the conduit of Herbert Eimert and Wolfgang Steinecke. Writing to Stockhausen almost immediately after his arrival, Eimert reveals that Steinecke 'wants to attempt to win Messiaen for this year's courses, but has no route to him whatsoever. Could such a connection be established by you via Goeyvaerts?'[42] Steinecke himself wrote to Goeyvaerts to this end one week later, in return offering a premiere of his Second Violin Concerto.[43] Goeyvaerts was clearly ambivalent and, in what retrospectively reads like an overplaying of his hand, suggests instead two performances of *Opus 2* separated by a pause, a formatting decision which 'is very important because the spiritual constitution which it [*Opus 2*] demands likely would not be established at a first hearing'.[44] The request appears to have cast doubt on Goeyvaerts's usefulness in Steinecke's mind, and he pursues the matter of Messiaen in correspondence with Stockhausen instead. Eager to please but having only just encountered Messiaen, Stockhausen in turn wrote to Goeyvaerts for information that he would pass on to Steinecke, with which Goeyvaerts obliged him cheerfully enough ('so viele Fragen zu beantworten!' begins a letter from 19 February 1952).[45]

Stockhausen's letters to Eimert from Paris reveal the influence of his Goeyvaerts–Messiaen orientation. In his first letter, after effusively thanking Eimert for 'so much and so unexpected help', Stockhausen encourages Eimert (and Steinecke) to bring only Messiaen instead of Jolivet to the 1952 Darmstadt courses, since 'the two have no connection whatsoever'.[46] This is a remarkable, if characteristic, self-assured statement from a young composer to a senior cultural administrator who had recently presented a work by Jolivet as representative of general progressive trends in New Music in his Darmstadt lecture with Steinecke. Eimert's view was certainly the more established one in the early 1950s, harmonising with Jean Étienne Marie's emplotment of Jolivet and Messiaen as the spiritual fathers of Boulez's practice.[47] Indeed, on either historical or aesthetic grounds, it is difficult to find any support for Stockhausen's claim, and it is very

[42] Eimert to Stockhausen, 11 January 1952. Quoted and translated in Iddon, *New Music at Darmstadt*, 71.

[43] Steinecke to Goeyvaerts, 18 January 1952. See Karel Goeyvaerts, *Selbstlose Musik: Texte • Briefe • Gespräche*, ed. Mark Delaere (Cologne: MusikTexte, 2010), 317.

[44] Goeyvaerts to Steinecke, 20 January 1952. Ibid., 298.

[45] 'So many questions to answer!' Goeyvaerts to Stockhausen, 19 February 1952; reproduced in Karel Goeyvaerts, *Selbstlose Musik: Texte • Briefe • Gespräche*, ed. Mark Delaere (Cologne: MusikTexte, 2010), 323.

[46] Stockhausen to Eimert, 18 January 1952; published in Helmut Kirchmeyer, 'Stockhausens Elektronische Messe nebst einem Vorspann unveröffentlichter Briefe aus seiner Pariser Zeit an Herbert Eimert', *Archiv für Musikwissenschaft*, 66.3 (2009), 234–5.

[47] Jean Étienne Marie, *Musique Vivante: Introduction au langage musical contemporain* (Paris: Editions Privat, 1953), 159–60.

likely that at this stage Stockhausen had no knowledge of Jolivet or his music. Nevertheless, Eimert (and, by extension, Steinecke) took Stockhausen's advice, and focused entirely on securing Messiaen for the 1952 courses.

Compared with his laconic submission to the 1951 Ferienkurse, Stockhausen took a distinctly more proactive approach with *Kreuzspiel*. As early as October 1951, he sent a handwritten copy of the score to Darmstadt for consideration in World New Music Days to be held in Salzburg.[48] The jury duly declared the piece 'unperformable', and, for the second year in a row, accepted pieces by Hans Werner Henze instead. A clearly embittered Stockhausen took issue with the evident aesthetic preferences of the jury, writing to Eimert: 'There's little point in getting gunpowder up one's arse like Mr Henze and exploding quite pitifully one day, subsequently flying around in outer space in a thousand pieces.'[49] Clearly, Stockhausen was undeterred, and through the help of Eimert and his slight leverage in the Messiaen wrangling, managed to make arrangements for two potential premieres by the end of January 1952, to take place either at the Frankfurt New Music Weeks or the 1952 Darmstadt courses. This was a savvy bit of competition which most likely nudged Steinecke towards offering a firm commitment for a performance in order to secure the premiere, despite his regarding the hiring of nine players as an extravagance.[50] While he was still doubtless among the youngest of the composers who would be present in 1952, Stockhausen's return to Darmstadt found him in a much more central and stable position within the courses. Furthermore, as his vitriol against Henze makes clear, Stockhausen believed he had found a trusted ally in Eimert.

Accordingly, something of a coherent, shared project soon becomes distinguishable in Stockhausen's correspondence with Eimert. By March 1952, Stockhausen was on friendly terms with Boulez, spurred not least by a mutual hatred of Henze (Stockhausen writes enthusiastically to Eimert: 'And how it stings when Boulez pounces on Henze – and everyone with him, wild with outrage: badly orchestrated, badly made, badly written, at last he is no musician, not even a commander of his métier').[51] The encounter with Boulez, like that with

---

[48] Iddon, *New Music at Darmstadt*, 70.

[49] 'Es hat wenig Sinn, Pulver in den Hintern zu kriegen wie Herr Henze und dann eines Tages ganz jämmerlich zu platzen, um so irgendwo im weiten Weltenraum herumzufliegen in tausend Stücken.' Stockhausen to Eimert, 1 February 1952; reproduced in Helmut Kirchmeyer, 'Stockhausens Elektronische Messe nebst einem Vorspann unveröffentlichter Briefe aus seiner Pariser Zeit an Herbert Eimert', *Archiv für Musikwissenschaft*, 66.3 (2009), 237. The above translation of this particularly difficult passage was suggested by Wieland Hoban.

[50] Iddon, *New Music at Darmstadt*, 71.

[51] 'Und wie weh tut das, wenn Boulez über Henze herfällt – und alle mit ihm, wild vor Entrüstung: schlecht orchestriert, schlecht gemacht, schlecht geschrieben, endlich ist er kein Musiker, nicht mal ein Beherrscher seines Metiers.' Stockhausen to Eimert, 10 March 1952; Kirchmeyer, 'Elektronische Messe', 239.

Goeyvaerts, reinforced Stockhausen's sense of having been denied access to his true calling within Germany's musical culture, and he insists that Eimert use his influence to remedy this situation: 'And I feel that you must make every effort to create a studio for M. Eppler [Werner Meyer-Eppler] or a chamber music series for young composers. And that is the only resource in all of Germany! It's well known in Paris that one can only accomplish anything in Cologne!'[52]

Clearly, Stockhausen had been inspired by the work that Boulez and Barraqué had been doing under Schaeffer's tutelage, as he mentions especially the interpolation and assembly of series for different parameters of sound – a clear overlap with what he had learned from Messiaen and Goeyvaerts.[53] However, Stockhausen clearly intends to deploy this technology towards far more Neo-Platonist ends than Boulez's series of timbres suggests. The echoes of Goeyvaerts's thinking are obvious:

> But personality is nevertheless expressed with this work, just the same as it is when using more traditional means. And finally, I believe that we are moving towards a time in which all material aspects (sonic broadening, searches for extraordinary effects, etc.) are increasingly subordinated to necessities manifest in the spiritual. No one wants to deny the tremendous possibilities of electronic music – but it is an expansion of the material breadth, which always quickly consumes itself, while the spiritual always demands the conservation of material.[54]

Within this spiritual scheme, Stockhausen takes Boulez for something of an enervated demiurge, who 'has a Satanic joy in destroying, in creating, in refining, in speculating and in debating'.[55] Indeed, it is precisely his preoccupation with the material sphere that precludes Boulez from the spiritual insights which Goeyvaerts's practice is able to attain:

> And so it is not surprising that he [Boulez] cannot make much of Goeyvaerts, who is ahead of us all, and whose last two works op. 2 and op. 3 (that Boulez, certainly, and no one else has encountered) are more than marvellous. (op. 2

---

[52] 'Und ich fühle es mit, wie Sie sich verrenken müssen, um ein Studio für M. Eppler oder eine Kammermusik-Reihe für die Jungen möglich zu machen. Und das ist die einzige Stelle in ganz Deutschland! Man weiß es sehr gut in Paris, daß nur in Köln was getan wird!' Ibid., 240.

[53] Stockhausen writes these names as 'Baraque' and 'Scheffer', which implies that he had not become well acquainted with either (see ibid.).

[54] 'Aber es ist eben so, daß sich bei dieser Arbeit die Persönlichkeit ebenso ausspricht, wie in der Handhabung überkommener Mittel. Und endlich glaube ich, daß wir in eine Zeit gehen, in der sich alle Materialaspekte (Klangliche Erweiterungen, Suchen nach außergewöhnlichen Effekten etc.) immer mehr den vom Geistigen ausgehenden Notwendigkeiten unterordnen. Niemand wird die ungeheueren Möglichkeiten der elektronischen Musik ableugnen wollen – aber es ist eine Erweiterung in die materialische Breite, die sich außerdem allemal schnell verbraucht, während das Geistige sich immer mehr auf Einsparung des Materialischen beruft.' Ibid.

[55] Ibid., 241.

will be performed this evening in Brussels – for 13 instruments – and he's still working on op. 3). In these two pieces I have been able to see, for the first time, onto the foundation of human comprehension, into the pure condensation of a musical idea. Try to seek out these, before all others, if my hearing tells you anything at all.[56]

In his turn, Steinecke offered Goeyvaerts a stipendium for the 1952 courses (recognising his having acted as a translator for Messiaen) but insisted on the performance of the Second Violin Concerto. After a few further attempts to push *Opus 2*, Goeyvaerts resigns himself to Steinecke's will, and requests that Steinecke forward the score of *Opus 2* Goeyvaerts had sent him to Alessandro Piovesan, the secretary of the Venice International Music Festival.[57] Responding to Steinecke's subsequent request for a programme note for the Darmstadt performance, Goeyvaerts minces neither words nor ambition:

> The Second Violin Concerto that is performed here still belongs to a series of orchestral and chamber music compositions whose aesthetics I have fully abandoned since 1950 [n.b. – the Second Violin Concerto was completed in January 1951 at the earliest]. There is still in this piece traditional twelve-tone technique and a rhythmic organisation based on 'series of note values' and timbres expressed through rhythmic 'personages'.
>
> New works are *Opus 1* for 2 pianos (a section of which was demonstrated in the Adorno Composition Seminar of the previous year), *Opus 2* for 13 Instruments and *Opus 3 with bowed and struck tones*. In these works the structure of each separate aspect of the sonic phenomenon is determined from a singular, timeless idea.
>
> Last year I had the opportunity to get to know the Darmstadt courses and concerts as a participant. I believe, that in our collectivist time, in which artistic production arises almost impersonally from the totality of the spiritual and is scarcely any expression of an individual feeling, these annual meetings, this exchange of thoughts fulfils an imperative necessity.[58]

---

[56] 'Und so ist es nicht verwunderlich, wenn er mit Goeyvaerts nicht viel anfangen kann, der uns allen voraus ist, und dessen letzten beiden Werke op. 2 und op. 3 (die Boulez allerdings und noch noch niemand nicht kennt) mehr als bewundernswert sind. (op. 2 wird heute abend uraufgeführt in Brüssel – für 13 Instrumente – und an op. 3 arbeitet er noch). In diesen beiden Stücken habe ich zum ersten Male auf den Grund des menschlich Begreifbaren sehen dürfen, in dem reinen Niederschlag einer musikalischen Idee. Versuchen sie es, diese zu bekommen vor allem anderen, wenn Ihnen mein Vernehmen irgend etwas sagt.' Ibid.

[57] Goeyvaerts to Steinecke, 3 May 1952. *Selbstlose Musik*, 300.

[58] 'Das Zweite Violinkonzert, das hier aufgeführt wird, gehört noch zu einer Reihe Orchester- und Kammermusikkompositionen, derer Ästhetik ich seit 1950 völlig aufgegeben habe. Es gibt in diesem Stück noch traditionelle Zwölftontechnik und eine rhythmische Organisation, die auf "Reihen von Notenwerten" und durch Klangfarbe ausgedrückte rhythmische "Personen" beruht. Neue Werke sind Opus 1 für 2 Klaviere (ein Satz davon wurde voriges Jahr im Adorno-Kompositionsseminar vorgeführt), Opus 2 für 13 Instrumente und Opus 3 mit angeschlagenen

Goeyvaerts's utopian longing for a communal Darmstadt was coupled with his dystopian experience of Flemish musical culture after his return from Paris. In a formulation that appears at its surface not a million miles off from the socially alienated artist of Adorno's modelling, Goeyvaerts writes to Stockhausen: 'You're right: it's patience that we need. If nothing comes and we remain in this horrible loneliness for a while, we become afraid and want to force the spirit out of this impasse. But more than ever, I know we must not do anything. The only thing we need is to wait and always keep faith.'[59] However, Goeyvaerts here feels himself to be not isolated from society at large, but removed from the particular network within which his practice functions. After his letter of introduction for Karlheinz, Goeyvaerts's correspondence with Jean Barraqué comes to an abrupt halt – Goeyvaerts tells Stockhausen in April 1952 that Barraqué never responded to this letter – and he appears increasingly reliant on his younger friend for information and conversation as well as professional exposure after a series of disappointments with both national and international musical authorities. [60] Goeyvaerts had become involved with the NIR (Nationaal Instituut voor de Radio-Omroep),[61] applying first for a job as a programmer (a job he ultimately did not get) and organising concerts with other Belgian composers like Louis De Meester, David Van de Woestijne, and Vic Legley, with whom he found little sympathy, kinship, or professional remuneration.[62]

---

und gestrichenen Tönen. In diesen Werken ist die Struktur bei jedem verschieden Aspekte der klanglichen Erscheinung von einer einzigen, zeitlosen Idee her bestimmt. In vorigen Jahr hatte ich Gelegenheit, die Darmstädter Ferienkurse und Konzerte als Teilnehmer kennenzulernen. Ich glaube, dass in unserer kollektivistischen Zeit, in der das künstlerische Schaffen fast unpersönlich aus der Totalität des Geistigen heraustritt und kaum mehr Ausdruck einer individuellen Empfindung ist, diese jährliche Zusammentreffen, dieser Austausch von Gedanken einer dringenden Notwendigkeit entspricht.' Goeyvaerts to Steinecke, 21 May 1952. *Selbstlose Musik*, 300.

[59] 'Tu as raison: c'est la patience qu'il nous faut. Si rien ne vient et l'on reste dans cette terrible solitude pendant quelque temps, alors on a peur et on veut forcer l'esprit à sortir de cette impasse. Mais plus que jamais, je sais qu'il ne faut rien faire. La seule chose qu'il faut c'est d'attendre et de garder toujours la foi.' Goeyvaerts to Stockhausen, 25 January 1952. *Selbstlose Musik*, 318–19. He nevertheless concludes in a distinctly non-Adornian vein: 'Il serait incompatible avec la bonté de Dieu de laisser attendre éternellement celui qui a soif de Sa Beauté.' ('It would be incompatible with God's loving kindness to let one thirsting for His beauty wait forever').

[60] Goeyvaerts to Stockhausen, 7 April 1952. *Selbstlose Musik*, 326–7.

[61] The NIR was absorbed into the BRT (Belgische Radio- en Televisieomroep) in 1960, which subsequently became the BRTN (Belgische Radio- en Televisieomroep Nederlandstalige Uitzendigen) in 1991, and, finally, the VRT (Vlaamse Radio- en Televisieomroeporganisatie) in 1998, which is still active today. See Lieve Desmet and Roel Vande Winkel, 'Historisch onderzoek naar de nieuwsproductie van de Vlaamse televisieomroep (NIR – BRT – BRTN – VRT): Een praktijkgebaseerde bronnenanalyse', *Belgisch Tijdschrift voor Nieuwste Geschiedenis/Revue Belge d'Histoire Contemporaine*, 39 (2009), 93–122.

[62] Karel Goeyvaerts, 'Paris – Darmstadt: 1947–1956: Excerpt from the Autobiographical Portrait', trans. Mark Delaere, *Revue belge de Musicologie/Belgisch Tijdschrift voor Muziekwetenschap*, 48 (1994), 47–8.

True to his word, Goeyvaerts kept patient and continued to compose. Sabbe describes *Opus 3 met gestreken en geslagen tonen*, composed during the first months of 1952, as achieving the 'ultimate form' that Goeyvaerts had been working towards in the Sonata and *Opus 2*.[63] Certainly this seems to be how Goeyvaerts must have thought of it, going by his description of the painful process of the work's completion to Stockhausen: 'it seems to me extremely difficult. Should it not be against the nature of music to be so difficult to invent? Or do all these difficulties come only from the fact that I am thinking too "humanly" to penetrate into these realms? One should think without *leading* their own thoughts.'[64] This artistic asceticism had by this point began to run parallel with a personal one, and Goeyvaerts immediately follows the description of his compositional problems with a complaint about the 'decadence' of Flanders, which drives him to distraction.

Accordingly, Goeyvaerts treated his activities in Belgium with detached ambivalence, which may have had a part in the scrapping of the planned concert premiere and radio broadcast of *Opus 2* (originally set for 4 and 2 June 1952, respectively, in Brussels).[65] If Stockhausen's encounter with Goeyvaerts suggested to him that Paris was the site of musical destiny, inversely, Goeyvaerts's encounter with Stockhausen appears to have convinced Goeyvaerts to set his hopes on Germany. This decision had mixed results. While Goeyvaerts's own initiatives to break into German musical life were largely unsuccessful – like that of Stockhausen, his submission (of *Opus 2*, naturally) to the Salzburg World New Music Days had been rejected –[66] his contact with Stockhausen and Eimert proved more fruitful, resulting in a radio broadcast of a studio recording of the Sonata for Two Pianos on NWDR-Köln.[67] This broadcast took place on 29 May 1952, on a programme that included the first performance of *Kreuzspiel* (likewise in a studio recording) and pieces by Messiaen (most likely

---

[63] Sabbe, 'Einheit', 14.

[64] 'Es scheint mir aber außerordentlich schwer. Soll es nicht gegen die Natur der Musik sein, sich so schwer erfinden zu lassen? Oder kommen alle diese Schwierigkeiten nur von der Tatsache, dass ich zu "menschlich" denke, um in diese Regionen vorzudringen? Man sollte denken, ohne sein eigenes Denken zu führen.' Goeyvaerts to Stockhausen, 22 January 1952. *Selbstlose Musik*, 317.

[65] Goeyvaerts to Stockhausen, 30 May 1952. *Selbstlose Musik*, 330–1.

[66] Goeyvaerts to Stockhausen, 25 January 1952. *Selbstlose Musik*, 318–19.

[67] This was preceded by a confusing episode: NWDR-Hamburg was to broadcast Goeyvaerts's Second Violin Concerto (a fact, omitted from Goeyvaerts's autobiography, that somewhat tempers his subsequent disavowals of the work) and were also interested in performing a 'new work' by him. Goeyvaerts sent them the Sonata at the same time that Stockhausen had given the score to Eimert as a suggestion for broadcast at NWDR-Köln. Unaware that the same work could not be performed at both stations, Goeyvaerts finally opted for broadcast on NWDR-Köln. Goeyvaerts to Stockhausen, 2 October 1951; *Selbstlose Musik*, 309–10. See also Goeyvaerts, 'Paris – Darmstadt', 49.

the *Quatre études de rhythme*) and Nono (perhaps a recording of *Polifonica-Monodia-Ritmica*, performed at the 1951 courses?) as well as a spoken introduction by Stockhausen describing the technical procedures involved in the composition of the works.[68] From Goeyvaerts's remarks, it is clear that Stockhausen's introduction presented the works as representing a unified tendency in contemporary composition, and his letter to Stockhausen demonstrates a concern that the connections between these different practices has not been made carefully or accurately: 'The Nono could have come first [in the programme], but then again there would be the difficulty of linking our music with that of Messiaen, which should occur at the beginning of the introduction.'[69] Goeyvaerts makes some minor objections to the performance of the Sonata, as well as the tone of Stockhausen's introduction: 'Maybe you were a bit too "technical" in your introductory words … but, sure … you can't always sacrifice everything for intelligibility.'[70]

While Stockhausen seems to have had a significant hand in the creation of this programme, the framing of the broadcast corresponds directly to the emplotment of New Music proposed by Eimert and Steinecke at the preceding Darmstadt courses, once again presenting an international group of young composers as central representatives of an objective historical tendency. The crucial difference was that here these international composers are placed within a single aesthetic category. Where Goeyvaerts's music was starkly contrasted with Nono's in 1951, now both composers, alongside Stockhausen, are deployed as a unified movement. Here was the way forward from the creative stalemate of the young composers that had been depicted by Eimert and Steinecke, one which neatly aligned with the blueprint they had presented less than a year prior, with some shuffling of parts (Messiaen has replaced Varèse as the major relevant composer of an older generation).

Judging by his comment on the broadcast, Goeyvaerts appears ambivalent about this new grouping, finding the Nono piece out of place in the programme and commenting that his sister's husband had 'quite spontaneously' remarked on the stark difference between the 'strong structure' of *Kreuzspiel* against Nono's music.[71] But for Stockhausen, and certainly for Eimert, the inclusion of Nono was a given. Stockhausen had written Nono on 10 March 1952, reminding

---

[68] There is very little information available on this broadcast; it is only given a parenthetical mention in Kurtz's Stockhausen biography.

[69] 'Der Nono hätte vielleicht zuerst kommen müssen, aber dann gäbe es wieder die Schwierigkeit, unsere Musik an die von Messiaen knüpfen, die doch am Anfang der Einführung vorkommen sollte.' Goeyvaerts to Stockhausen, 30 May 1952. *Selbstlose Musik*, 330–1.

[70] 'Vielleicht warst Du in Deinen einführenden Worten ein bisschen zu "technisch" … Aber, ja … Man kann doch nicht immer alles der Verständlichkeit opfern.' Ibid.

[71] Ibid.

him of their 'brief encounter at Darmstadt'.[72] Stockhausen informed Eimert that
he had formally contacted his Italian peer: 'I've written to Nono – introduced
myself to him, as it were.'[73] Nevertheless, Nono wrote back enthusiastically and
almost immediately (13 March), professing not only remembrance of
Stockhausen but deep kinship with him and Goeyvaerts (who Nono repeatedly
refers to collectively with Stockhausen), focused particularly in Darmstadt
itself:

> I believe that you and Goeyvaerts are like me and Maderna. When we work
> and live together, I believe something genuinely good and beautiful can be
> achieved musically. At the Marienhöhe we will see together, clearly, how and
> with whom it can be done. It must be a brotherhood; if something is done
> against one of us, it will be as if it were done against all of us.[74]

Soon after, Nono also made friendly overtures to Goeyvaerts in a letter
Stockhausen's wife passed on to the composer in Antwerp (Nono had eviden-
tially written the letter before asking for Goeyvaerts's address, or assumed that
Goeyvaerts lived with Stockhausen, and had sent it directly to Stockhausen).[75]
Writing to Stockhausen in response, Goeyvaerts was appreciative of Nono's
letter more for its ethical dimension than its overtures of artistic commonality.
In fact, Goeyvaerts draws a sharp distinction between Nono and 'young
Frenchmen' like Boulez and Barraqué: '[Nono] is indeed quite nice and
seems to be upright to me (so much different than Barraqué, Boulez, etc.). His
suggestion for candid [*offenherzig*] criticism is so honourable and much different than the young Frenchmen, who always give free rein to annihilation in their
criticism of friends.'[76] Goeyvaerts's opinion of Nono here is nothing new. In
a letter addressed to Barraqué during the 1951 Ferienkurse, Goeyvaerts writes:
'One of the finest, nicest, and most cultured fellows is the young Italian Luigi
Nono. I am curious to hear his music.'[77] It remains to be seen, then, what had
motivated these composers to connect in such a 'brotherhood' at this point in

---

[72] Stockhausen to Nono, 10 March 1952, in *Karlheinz Stockhausen bei den Internationalen Ferienkursen für Neue Musik Darmstadt 1951–1996: Dokumente und Briefe*, ed. Imke Misch and Markus Bandur (Kürten: Stockhausen, 2001), 39; quoted and translated in Iddon, *New Music at Darmstadt*, 71.

[73] 'An Nono habe ich geschrieben – mich sozusagen vorgestellt.' Stockhausen to Eimert, 10 March 1952; Kirchmeyer, 'Elektronische Messe', 241.

[74] Nono to Stockhausen, 13 March 1952, in *Karlheinz Stockhausen bei den Internationalen Ferienkursen*, 41; quoted and translated in Iddon, *New Music at Darmstadt*, 72.

[75] Goeyvaerts to Doris Stockhausen, 28 March 1951. *Selbstlose Musik*, 325.

[76] 'Er ist tatsächlich ganz nett und scheint mir rechtschaffen zu sein (so ganz anders als Barraqué, Boulez, usw.). Sein Vorschlag zur offenherzigen Kritik ist so ehrlich und ganz anders als die jungen Franzosen, die in ihrer Kritik ihrer Freunde an der Vernichtung immer freien Lauf lassen.' Goeyvaerts to [Karlheinz] Stockhausen, 28 March 1951. *Selbstlose Musik*, 324–5.

[77] 'Un des gens fins, des plus gentils, des plus cultivés est le jeune italien Luigi Nono. Je suis curieux d'entendre sa musique.' Goeyvaerts to Barraqué, 29 June 1951. *Selbstlose Musik*, 284.

spring 1952, rather than immediately following their initial encounter in Darmstadt.

3.2 Eimert's *Lehrbuch*

Alongside Maderna, Nono had already visited Eimert in early 1952, during which time they undertook intensive study of twelve-tone technique, and it is likely that Stockhausen received Nono's address from Eimert in the first place.[78] As Iddon suggests, this was almost certainly under the auspices of Eimert's recent *Lehrbuch der Zwölftontechnik*.[79] The book had initially been published in 1950 by Breitkopf and presents an intensely structural focus on row construction and its compositional applications. Like Rufer's, Eimert's scope is ecumenical, and, while foregrounding his argument on works by Schoenberg, Berg, and Webern, draws from a broad range of musical production. Unlike Rufer, these composers are never designated as a 'school' – Eimert instead refers to a 'Schoenberg circle' in Vienna.[80] Nevertheless, Eimert thoroughly, even self-consciously, adopts the Adornian-Leibowitzian historicist model. Twelve-tone music is 'firmly situated in music-historical development [*Gefüge*], a last, generalised material process of music which at its core has nothing whatsoever to do with modish and topical stylistic tendencies', whose relevance is comparable to 'the polyphonic epoch' of Bach or the 'figured bass age' of Monteverdi.[81]

While Iddon characterises Eimert as a Josef Matthias Hauer partisan, the position Eimert advocates in his *Lehrbuch* is at once far more broad, more complex, and more totalising than that of Heiß or Steinbauer.[82] Eimert foregrounds not only Schoenberg and Hauer (and Krenek) as the sources of twelve-tone technique, but prominently his teacher Jef Golyscheff, twice citing articles by Willi Schuh describing Golyscheff in the context of Mann's *Doktor Faustus*.[83] As he echoes the conclusions of the twelve-tone congresses

---

[78] Iddon, *New Music at Darmstadt*, 72.   [79] Ibid.

[80] See, for example, Eimert, *Lehrbuch der Zwölftontechnik* (Wiesbaden: Breitkopf & Härtel, 1952), 58–9. Even in this case, Eimert is careful to differentiate between Schoenberg, Berg, and Webern.

[81] Ibid., 5.   [82] See Iddon, *New Music at Darmstadt*, 92–3.

[83] Eimert, *Lehrbuch*, 57. To reduce ambiguity, Eimert's spelling of 'Jef Golyscheff' is retained. It is worth mentioning in passing that Golyscheff himself might well have taken issue with Eimert's totalising deployment of his formal experiments, which arose in the context of the avowed Dadaism of the Novembergruppe. In contrast to Eimert's, art critic Adolf Behne's understanding of Golyscheff's practice in 1919 explicitly eschews structural analysis in favour of an emancipated anti-historicism: 'Seriousness is the ancestral, the grandfatherly, the spurious, the retrograde, the dull-witted. . . . The foremost work today must be: *cheerfulness!* . . . [Golyscheff] will bring joy and redeem cheerfulness.' See Adolf Behne, 'Werkstattbesuche II. Jefim Golyshceff', *Der Cicerone*, 9.22 (1919); quoted in Eckhard John, *Musik-Bolschewismus: Die Politisierung der Musik im Deutschland 1918–1938* (Stuttgart: J. B. Metzler, 1994), 144.

(where, in 1951, he himself gave a talk debating 'Twelve-Tone Style or Twelve-Tone Technique?'),[84] twelve-tone technique for Eimert is precisely that: a constructive basis for the ordering of musical material. In Eimert's telling, the blinkered aesthetic focus of critics like Hans Ferdinand Redlich and Adorno threatens to calcify exactly the historical potential and technical possibilities of this technique by telescoping it as merely a particularised and impoverished enunciation of an objective historical condition which has long passed: 'music-theoretical understanding has remained utterly stuck in the primitive beginnings of those *Anbruch* essays'.[85] While this is nominally a riposte directed at Adorno, here Eimert in fact explodes Adorno's historicist model into a universal programme, in which twelve-tone technique is generalised as the transcendent signifier of New Music through an analytical *Aufhebung* of the Second Viennese School.

The cataloguing impulse which undergirds this book, replete with row tables, diagrams, and charts of intervallic structures, in retrospect seems to have much in common with similar arguments advanced by Milton Babbitt (the attention given to the intervallic character of row forms and their corresponding *Gestalt* particularly prefiguring combinatoriality and, by extension, pitch-class set theory); its repeated emphasis of possibilities for 'polyphony', conversely, seems to place it closer to a French (read: post-Leibowitz) understanding of twelve-tone techniques. However, some of Eimert's formulations seem to be reminiscent of the structural devices deployed by Goeyvaerts, Barraqué, and Messiaen – certainly they would have appeared so to a young composer eagerly adopting this practice.

In a discussion of all-interval series (which appears to be indebted equally to F. H. Klein and Berg's 'grandmother chord' and to Webern's structural segmentation of rows), Eimert describes a symmetrical series divided by a tritone at its centre. Similarly, in a later chapter on 'Series-Refractions (Non-Twelve-Tone Thematic)', Eimert describes three strategies for 'refracting' series to arrive at 'non-twelve-tone themes':

1. through harmonic or polyphonic refracting of a series;
2. through crossing of series;
3. through interpolation of different series.[86]

---

[84] *Im Zenit der Moderne*, III.548.

[85] ' ... merkwürdigerweise aber ist die musiktheoretische Erkenntnis ganz in dem primitiven Anfängen der ersten "Anbruch"-Aufsätze steckengeblieben'. Eimert, *Lehrbuch*, 59. Eimert is here referring to the Schoenberg volume of the journal *Anbruch*, published in 1924, and in particular Erwin Stein's essay 'Neue Formprinzipien'.

[86] Ibid., 45.

Eimert's explanation of the second item in this inventory as a mirror-symmetrical exchange of rows suggests a smaller-scale version of the structural devices used in Goeyvaerts's Sonata and *Kreuzspiel*. Similarities notwithstanding, the possible theological dimensions of these structures are not touched on in either case, and Eimert moves briskly onwards to cataloguing further aspects of row organisation.

Eimert republished *Lehrbuch der Zwölftontechnik* two years later, in 1952, with a new 'Supplement' which both greatly expands the scope of Eimert's historical framework and clarifies its trajectory. Expanding on the 'series-refractions' discussed in the first edition, Eimert proposes such refractions within a single row. The reason for giving this new demonstration, Eimert explains, is that 'it very easily reveals the way to the constructive method of completely through-organised [*durchorganisierten*] material'.[87] This is precisely the path which Richard Toop retroactively attempts to map in his emplotment moving from the *durchgeordnete Musik* of Messiaen, Goeyvaerts, and Fano, to the 'proper' serialism of Boulez and Stockhausen.[88] Writing twenty years earlier, the trajectory of this path seems just as clear to Eimert. After a cursory mention of 'new contributions' such as Krenek's '"Rotation"-principle of row segments', Eimert turns to a more important matter: 'Compared with this, for the first time something fundamentally new has developed in the thinking developed in Messiaen's school, which applies the variation principle to all dimensions of sound material.'[89] In retrospect, this reads as a fairly *de rigueur* assessment of the development of post-war serialism, one echoed by both specialised (e.g. Toop) and general scholarship dealing with the foundation of the Darmstadt School. In 1952, however, there are at least three unique, consolidating claims advanced by Eimert here. First, and most obviously, the development of this idea is 'fundamentally [*grundsätzlich*] new' when seen against general historical tendencies since the advent of the twelve-tone system, reducing practices like that of Krenek to imitative dilettantism. Second, Messiaen has here for the first time been given that subject position of primary historical priority in the Adornian-Leibowitzian schema of international-institutional New Music: he is the leader of a school. Third, in contravention to Messiaen's own ambivalence towards twelve-tone music in general and Schoenberg in particular, this new Messiaenic school is brought into line

---

[87] Ibid., 61.

[88] Richard Toop, 'Messiaen/Goeyvaerts, Fano/Stockhausen, Boulez', *Perspectives of New Music*, 13.1 (1974), 141–69.

[89] 'Zum ersten mal etwas grundsätzlich Neues dagegen enthält der in der Schule Messiaens entwickelte Gedanke, das Variations-prinzip auf alle Dimensionen der Tonmaterie anzuwenden.' Ibid.

with the continuum of Adornian-Leibowitzian historicism as the historically necessary, ineluctable progression of the structuring of musical material.

It is this last claim that necessitates Eimert's concept of the 'variation principle'. Within the Adornian-Leibowitzian model, this is precisely the method by which Schoenberg secured historical legitimacy for his twelve-tone practice, against the anti-historical no man's land of barren asceticism: 'By contrast [to Hauer], Schoenberg radically integrates the classical, and, even more, the archaic techniques of variation into twelve-tone material.'[90] However, none of the composers of Messiaen's newly christened school – least of all Messiaen himself – had any sustained compositional engagement with nor even interest in such a 'variation principle' as a formal device. It is broadly true that certain students of Messiaen – Barraqué, Goeyvaerts, Michel Fano, Stockhausen – differentiated multiple aspects (not yet the more familiarly scientistic 'parameters') of a composition and treated them separately before re-combining them within a single global schema. However, the formal procedures these composers applied to the separated compositional aspects bear little resemblance to any method of classical variation. Quite the opposite: the pursuit of a 'static music' which occupied these composers at this time necessitated formal procedures which minimised, even annihilated any suggestion of dynamism or fluidity in order to more perfectly enunciate a trace of absolute Being.

Yet Eimert insists on the centrality of this variation principle: 'As the classical procedure of twelve-tone technique related only to melody and harmony, thus now the other elements of music follow the variation principle of constant transformation prefigured in twelve-tone technique.'[91] Characteristically, Eimert gives a list of these elements:

1. the twelve tones,
2. the octave registers (up to seven),
3. the different rhythmic values,
4. the different levels of dynamic intensity,
5. the characteristic articulation (attack) form of the tone (staccato, tenuto, legato, etc.).[92]

In an addendum which belatedly answers Adorno's question on where antecedent and consequent phrasing figures in with all this, Eimert explains: 'For

---

[90] Theodor Adorno, *Philosophy of New Music*, trans. Robert Hullot-Kentor (Minneapolis: University of Minnesota Press, 2006), 45.

[91] 'Bezog sich das klassische Verfahren der Zwölftontechnik nur auf die Melodik und Harmonik, so folgen nun auch die anderen Elemente der Musik dem in der Zwölftontechnik vorgebildeten Variationsprinzip des ständigen Wechsels.' Eimert, *Lehrbuch*, 61.

[92] Ibid., 61–2.

the structure of the phrase, the evaluation of octave registers – which already with Anton Webern has led to broadly spaced "punctual" formations – is critical.'[93]

Taken together, these three claims consolidate and advance the project outlined by Eimert and Steinecke: the proposal of a new phase of the international avant-garde which synthesised historically determined technical procedures of dodecaphony with an expanded inventory of musical material and, subsequently, transcended the impasse (or 'limit-situation') of Schoenbergian dodecaphony. Accordingly, Eimert's argument here pushes Messiaen, Goeyvaerts, and Stockhausen into a teleological history which reads their practice as the necessary fulfilment of the formal potential of Schoenberg and Webern, subtly reconciled with the (now unnamed) Josef Matthias Hauer: 'It appears that something has been fulfilled here which was already anticipated right at the beginning of twelve-tone music [*Zwölftonmusik*], at the antipode of Schoenbergian affect-music: the free, balanced twelve-tone game [*Zwölftonspiel*], which is arrived at by the way of the autonomous combinatorial experiment.'[94] In short, Eimert reads Messiaen, Goeyvaerts, and Stockhausen on Adorno's terms, which is to say that he articulates their practices within a formal vocabulary that can be assimilated into the discourse of institutional New Music – precisely what Goeyvaerts and Stockhausen failed to do in July 1951.

The argument of Eimert's supplement, which proposes for the first time an aesthetic kinship between an international group of young composers and certain formal procedures developed by Olivier Messiaen, matches up neatly to Goeyvaerts's account of Stockhausen's introduction to the radio programme which included *Kreuzspiel* and the Sonata. Indeed, Eimert even provides a musical example which reads as a hybrid between these two pieces, using 'the twelve pitches, six octave registers, six rhythmic values (semiquaver, quaver, crotchet within a triplet with quaver rest, crotchet, dotted crotchet, minim), five dynamic values (pianissimo, piano, mezzo-forte, forte, fortissimo) and three characteristic attack forms (stacc., ten., leg.)'.

The resulting four bars notated on a grand stave (see Figure 1) look a great deal like the piano parts in the Sonata or *Kreuzspiel*, and Eimert's description of where the music might go from here is equally familiar:

---

[93] 'Für die Struktur des Tonsatzes wird die Auswertung der Oktavlagen entscheidend, die schon bei Anton Webern zu weiträumigen "punktuellen" Bildungen geführt hat.' Ibid., 62.

[94] 'Hier scheint sich etwas zu erfüllen, was schon ganz in den Anfängen der Zwölftonmusik, am Gegenpol der Schönbergschen Affektmusik, geahnt wurde: das freie ausgeglichene Zwölftonspiel, das auf dem Wege des autonomen kombinatorischen Experiments gewonnen wird.' Ibid., 63. This is specifically in reference to Messiaen's 'Quatre Etudes for piano [*sic*]', which Eimert dates to 1951.

Figure 1 Demonstration of 'punctual' music in Eimert, *Lehrbuch der Zwölftontechnik,* 62 (ex. 84)

This is the first phase of a piece [wherein] the pitches are distributed so that each of the six octave registers contains two of the twelve pitches. According to the plan of construction, the tones must now be passed through the octave registers in the following phases. The example could just as well represent the end phase; the beginning phase would then look like a twelve-tone sequence in a tight register, from which the pitches would be led out from phase to phase and distributed to the other octave registers.[95]

With regards to the other 'elements' of the composition, Eimert's text borrows even more explicitly from the practice of the younger musicians: 'Rhythm, dynamics, and attack forms are similarly brought into a fixed ordering condition, such that they are all related to a synthetic number of order that remains fixed throughout the phases.'[96] Unquestionably, this is a programmatic technical demonstration of the compositional procedures involved in *Kreuzspiel*, the Sonata, and, to a lesser extent, Messiaen's *Quatre études de rythme*, the only piece of music which Eimert refers to by title in the text. Indeed, Goeyvaerts's particular objection to the 'technical' quality of the programme's introduction suggests that it was not Stockhausen at all who had written it, but Eimert. Even if Stockhausen had not been directly ventriloquised by Eimert in this case, the text of this supplement demonstrates that Eimert was certainly prepared to incorporate wholesale, and generalise, specific technical procedures from the practices of younger composers into his master narrative of New Music. This is hugely significant: 'synthetic

---

[95] 'Das ist die erste Phase eines Stückes, gewissermaßen die "Grundreihe" des doppelten Verfahrens mit den Tönen und den Oktavlagen. In diesem Fall sind die Töne so verteilt, daß jede der sechs Oktavlagen zwei von den zwölf Tönen enthält. Nach dem Konstruktionsplan müssen die Töne nun in den folgenden Phasen durch die Oktavlagen geführt werden. Das Beispiel könnte ebensogut die Schlußphase verkörpern; die Anfangsphase sähe dann etwa so aus wie eine Zwölftonfolge in enger Lage, aus der die Töne dann Phase um Phase herausgeführt und auf die übrigen Oktavlagen verteilt werden müßten.' Ibid., 62.

[96] 'Auch Rhythmus, Dynamik und Anschlagsform sind in ein festes Ordnungsverhältnis zu bringen, und zwar so, da sie alle auf eine synthetische Ordnungszahl bezogen werden, die durch alle Phase hindurch festgehalten wird.' Ibid., 63.

number', a compositional device devised by Karel Goeyvaerts and consistently applied only by him, is taken to be representative of not only a large international group of composers but the acme of technical progress in art music.

Goeyvaerts's 'technical' objection, as well as his pointed observation about Nono's fundamental difference, highlight the effect of this move and its departure from what Goeyvaerts understands his music to be. Eimert has effectively transformed the particularly Roman Catholic metaphysical programme of this practice into a universalised technical schema, one which follows organically on the heels of dodecaphony as an internationally valid method of composition. The formal procedures utilised by Goeyvaerts and Stockhausen to arrive at an approximation of a selfless music wherein pure being (the Absolute, Roman Catholic deity) is momentarily made present have, in Eimert's new emplotment, become the inverse: the next historically logical step in a dialectical process of increasing mastery over musical material, the way out of the limit-situation imposed by the advent of twelve-tone music. As such, they are now no longer in the service of the Roman Catholic God but the dialectical-materialist History of Adorno and Leibowitz – the conceptual as well as the practical prerequisite for the Darmstadt School. Indeed, Eimert's elevation of this practice into Adornian-Leibowitzian institutional discourse circumscribes its descriptive and legitim-ising vocabulary. By replacing its Neo-Platonic frame with a historicist one, this practice is universalised as a world-historical condition – one which overlaps neatly with the contemporary institutional ideology of New Music.

There is an additional, subtler discursive transferral enacted in this replace-ment. While Eimert's new emplotment incorporates the pre-compositional methods of this practice wholesale, to the point of near plagiarism in the case of 'synthetic number', his reading of the technical operations themselves, shorn of their Neo-Platonist numerology, is rather more mechanistic. To begin with, Eimert's composer is given free rein to organise each divisible compositional element in whichever configuration might be more compelling. There is no reason to prefer a cross-structure to, say, a rhapsodic structure in combining the separate compositional parameters; even his interpretation of the unifying 'synthetic number' is thoroughly secular. Such a reading emphasises process rather than stasis, describing the constructive means by which elements are progressively recombined rather than a unifying system for fixing their appear-ance in an immutable order that mirrors some sort of higher being. This, then, is the crucial difference between Eimert's 'punctual music' and Goeyvaerts's 'static music' – it is a depiction of a mechanical procedure rather than a metaphysical state. Accordingly, it is generalised. Eimert's reading of Goeyvaerts and Stockhausen's practice not only brings it into line with the operative institutional historicism but aligns it with numerous other composers, such as Boulez, Leibowitz, Nono, and Maderna, who had similarly applied twelve-tone procedures to other musical parameters. While all these practices were previously disparate, arising from mutually exclusive aesthetic concerns and ideological traditions – and, in Stockhausen and Goeyvaerts's case, only remotely related to the music of Schoenberg, Berg, or Webern – Eimert's technical reading emphasises their unity and universal application in New Music as the Darmstadt School of post-Webernian punctual music.

Indeed, the category of 'punctual music' itself is far from self-evident, since no practitioner associated with the category had described their work in such terms. According to Wörner, Eimert 'hit upon the word *punktuell*' in conversation with Stockhausen over Messiaen's 'Mode' at some unspecified later date after Golea's Darmstadt lecture in 1951.[97] Kirchmeyer fixes the date of the coinage at 30 December 1952, in a letter from Eimert to Stockhausen;[98] Wörner's suggestion appears more plausible since, as noted above, Eimert was deploying *punktuell* to describe Webernian figurations throughout 1952. At any rate, it is a rather more technical and sober classification than 'static music' or 'fantastic music of the stars', and thus appears to be a characteristic Eimertism. But such a category of music, existing on the vanguard of technical proficiency and defined by the careful, isolated consideration of each of its constituent elements, had already been devised by Eimert in 1925. Eimert's term then was not *punktuell* but *atomistisch*, and he categorised recent works by Schoenberg, Hauer, and Golyscheff as 'atomistic music', a tradition within which he placed his own compositional output.[99]

Here something of the historical contingency of Eimert's position becomes visible. Eimert's first theoretical publication, the *Atonale Musiklehre*, published while he was still a student at the Cologne Musikhochschule in 1924, is very similar to the later *Lehrbuch* in both style and content, with the main body of the text largely devoted to inventories of technical elements (in particular, various configurations of 'twelve-tone complexes', a term borrowed from Golyscheff). In the second section of the tract, subtitled 'Historical and Aesthetic Observations', Eimert outlines a vague teleology of musical development, beginning with 'the classical view of centricity (root, tonality)' and concluding with 'the loosening of tonally-organized harmony in Impressionism'.[100] However, Eimert explicitly

---

[97] Karl H. Wörner, *Stockhausen: Life and Work*, trans. Bill Hopkins (Berkeley: University of California Press, 1973), 80–2.

[98] Kirchmeyer, *Kleine Monographie über Herbert Eimert* (Leipzig: Sächsischen Akademie der Wissenschaften, 1998), 41 (endnote 93).

[99] Ibid., 11 (see also endnote 87).

[100] Eimert, *Atonale Musiklehre*, translated in Jennifer L. Weaver, 'Theorizing Atonality: Herbert Eimert's and Jefim Golyscheff's Contributions to Composing with Twelve Tones' (unpublished PhD thesis, University of North Texas, 2014), 61.

rejects this tradition as irrelevant to the topic at hand because it has manifestly failed to come to grips with the empirical technical means of music: 'When attempting a theoretical groundwork of Impressionism, one immediately encounters the un-mergable opposition of music-logical and aural-psychological functions.'[101] In opposition to this historical teleology, Eimert proposes a purely technical one: 'The development from classical to modern music is a constantly progressing compression and spatial reduction of the seven-tone tonal complexes by the means of modulation.'[102] The implications of these 'technical foundations' are explored throughout the remainder of the section, with both the systematic impulse and Eimert's contribution to it clearly foregrounded: 'In 1914, twelve-tone music was found for the first time in the unpublished compositions of the Russian Golyscheff. Some years later, the idea of pure atonality took on a tangible form with the Viennese theorist and composer Hauer. Within this developmental line, this current musical treatise provides the first systematic presentation of atonal techniques.'[103] In this light, Eimert's continuing interventions within the evolving discourse of New Music appear to have been made from a remarkably consistent ideological position for almost four decades: even before the advent of 'punctual music', he had insisted on the primacy of the technical universality of twelve-tone technique, most notably in his contribution to the Second International Twelve-Tone Congress in Darmstadt in 1951. Indeed, Eimert's reading of Golyscheff (and, to a lesser extent, Hauer) in the *Atonale Musiklehre* proposes precisely what he later put forward in his reading of Stockhausen, Goeyvaerts, Messaien, and, above all, Webern: a total rational configuration of parametrised technical means of composition.

3.3 *Kreuzspiel* and Its Aftermath

Taking a broad view of the programme, there is little to suggest that the 1952 Darmstädter Ferienkurse offered anything radically new or different from their previous iterations. The courses opened with a performance of Jean Giraudoux's *Judith* with incidental music by Henze, followed by staged performances of Orff's *Die Kluge* (1942), which had previously been staged at the 1946 courses, and Honegger's *Jeanne d'Arc au bûcher* (1934–1935); over the course of the following week, Heinrich Strobel presented a six-part lecture series on 'the complete works of Igor Stravinsky', a subject on which he had also lectured in 1947.[104] The concert schedule included works by Prokofiev, Leibowitz, Dallapiccola, Stravinsky, Bartók, Milhaud, Ravel, Jolivet, Hindemith, and

---

[101] Ibid., 62.

[102] Ibid., 63. Eimert goes on to cite 'the investigations of Stumpf and Riemann' as disproving Helmholtz's assertion of the phenomenological role of the overtone series (ibid., 64).

[103] Ibid., 66.   [104] *Im Zenit der Moderne*, III.552–7.

Jacques Ibert, alongside those of Schoenberg, Berg, and Webern, with further portrait concerts devoted to Bartók and Ferruccio Busoni. Indeed, this compositional roster for officially scheduled concerts remained largely unchanged throughout the 1950s.

It would appear, then, that Eimert's blueprint for the Darmstadt School – not to mention Leibowitz and Adorno's earlier blueprint for New Music – was totalising in content but not effect. Judging from scheduled performances and lectures alone, certainly there is little indication of any fundamental change in the state of affairs which had existed since 1946 (repeat performances of Orff, repeat lectures on Stravinsky, etc.). There are, nevertheless, a few indications which point towards the unified Darmstadt School of music historiography. Most obviously, there was the presence of Messiaen, who led composition seminars alongside Hanns Jelinek and performed his *Quatre études de rythme* in the opening concert (with Jelinek's Second String Quartet). Less obviously, the concerts devoted to 'music of the young generation' – a feature of the courses since 1948; previous iterations mentioned 'new' or 'contemporary music' *tout court* – for the first time brought together most of the foundational figures of the Darmstadt School (Pierre Boulez, Karlheinz Stockhausen, Karel Goeyvaerts, Bruno Maderna, and Luigi Nono) alongside what amount to 'bit players' in Darmstadt historiography, such as Giselher Klebe and Renzo Dall'Oglio.[105] To be sure, this music in total represented less than 5 per cent of the programmed concerts (in terms of duration of the performances, even less). Nevertheless, it was these performances, and the so-called Wunderkonzert on 21 July 1952 containing *Kreuzspiel* in particular, which were reliably the focus of critical reception both in 1952 and subsequently. Eimert's blueprint was only tangentially concerned with the actual programming of Darmstadt – like that of Adorno and Leibowitz, it was primarily occupied with the discourse of New Music.

Certainly, it was in a discursive capacity that Eimert's presence was central to the 1952 courses. While it had nowhere near the breadth of Strobel's Stravinsky panorama, Eimert's lecture on 'Problems of Electronic Music' gave a concentrated crash course in the new teleology he had developed, which presently resulted in both 'punctual music' and electronic music. Indeed, Eimert suggests, the two are inseparable at the zenith of New Music practice, since through punctual music 'the connection to electronic possibilities is quite automatic'.[106] The technical means

[105] The term 'bit players' has been used by Iddon to describe figures like Pousseur and Goeyvaerts; see Iddon, 'Die zufälligen Serialisten – oder: Die Darmstädter Schule und wie es dazu kam', lecture given at Darmstadt, 12 August 2014.

[106] Eimert, 'Probleme der elektronischen Musik', Darmstadt, 21 July 1952; quoted in Hans Heinrich Eggebrecht, 'Punktuelle Musik', in *Terminologie der Musik im 20. Jahrhundert*, ed. Hans Heinrich Eggebrecht (Stuttgart: Franz Steiner, 1995), 353.

which underlie this connection, as well as their historical derivation, are those which Eimert delineated in his *Lehrbuch*: the total rational configuration of parametrised technical means of composition which arose from the practice of Anton Webern. Eggebrecht summarises the positioning of Eimert's move very neatly: 'The expression "punctual music" casually functions as a connecting concept to electronic music, above all as a bridging concept from serial music back to Webern; through this he conveniently provides historical legitimation to serial music.'[107] But here Eimert applies this point directly to the discursive reception of New Music, addressing his Darmstadt audience directly and instructing them that 'wherever you hear this peculiar punctual music, the spirit of Webern is present that has indeed pre-shaped the idea of totally through-organised [*durchorganisierten*] musical material'.[108] Considering that this instruction was given less than five hours before the scheduled performance of *Kreuzspiel*, Eimert's invocation of 'wherever' appears rather directed.

Irrespective of his new status as a member of the embryotic Darmstadt School, Goeyvaerts once again does not appear to have enjoyed his stay at the courses. While it may have been some small comfort that he no longer had to share a room with Jacques Wildberger, Wildberger was nevertheless present – in fact, his Quartet for flute, clarinet, violin, and cello had been programmed alongside *Kreuzspiel*. This must have stung Goeyvaerts, who had previously entertained hopes that both *Kreuzspiel* and *Opus 2* might be performed in the same concert.[109] His repeated appeals to Stockhausen to have Steinecke recruit Yvette Grimaud to perform instead of the despised Yvonne Loriod ('please tell him that the only pianist who has developed a relevant playing technique of New Music is called Yvette Grimaud') were either ineffective or ignored, and Loriod in fact was further engaged to lead a piano seminar.[110] Worse still, Goeyvaerts was further humiliated by being recruited to page turn for Loriod's performance of Boulez's Second Sonata, a fact he bitterly remembered thirty years later.[111] His further recollection of Yvonne turning to him after the concert and announcing the 'two revelations of the moment' as Stockhausen and Boulez appears somewhat more doubtful, if no less earnest.[112] But it was the Wunderkonzert and its aftermath that seems to have hurt Goeyvaerts the most. While Goeyvaerts gives no recollection of the concert itself in his

---

[107] 'Der Ausdruck punktuelle Musik fungiert gelegentlich als Anschlußbegriff zur elektronischen Musik, vor allem über als Brückenbegriff von der seriellen Musik zurück zu Webern; dadurch ist er geeignet, die serielle Musik geschichtlich zu legitimieren.' Eggebrecht, 'Punktuelle Musik', 353 (formatting altered).

[108] Eimert, 'Probleme', in ibid., 353.

[109] Goeyvaerts to Stockhausen, 16 November 1951. *Selbstlose Musik*, 311–12.

[110] Goeyvaerts to Stockhausen, 19 February 1952.   [111] Goeyvaerts, 'Paris – Darmstadt', 49.

[112] Ibid.

memoir, he does mention a dinner after the courses with Stockhausen and his wife Doris, hosted by Doris's uncle, at which 'Karlheinz could not stop talking about the sensation created by *Kreuzspiel*.' When Doris's uncle inquires if any of Goeyvaerts's music had been performed, Stockhausen responded 'Sure, with an orchestra.'[113] Little wonder, then, that Goeyvaerts decided to bid the summer courses good riddance: 'For me that ended Darmstadt. I have never been back.'[114]

The live premiere of *Kreuzspiel* had indeed generated attention. In fact, the public scandal of *Kreuzspiel* was explicitly connected to the classroom scandal of the previous year, with Stockhausen again serving as the famulus of a rigidly esoteric musical practice. However, while the confrontation with Adorno by all accounts was conceptually bewildering and unexpected, the Darmstadt community was well prepared for its encounter with *Kreuzspiel*. In a review by Albert Rodemann for the *Darmstädter Tagesblatt,* which Iddon characterises as 'probably about the norm' for press response, the grouping is explicit:

> Why Karl Heinz [*sic*] Stockhausen entitled his music for oboe, bass clarinet, piano, and four percussionists *Kreuzspiel* is incomprehensible. Following a system of 'static music', the indefensibleness of which Theodor Adorno already demonstrated the previous year to its Flemish inventor, the sound of the piece goes far beyond that which we have been accustomed to call music. That he [n. b. – this refers to Goeyvaerts, not Stockhausen] finds a few devotees to celebrate his work ... doesn't change things a jot. Every idea finds its prophets. And its sect.[115]

The ideological priming shaping Rodemann's account is twofold. On one layer, there is the familiar concept of the quasi-Gnostic 'sect', the negative antecedent of the proper 'school' grouping of historically legitimate New Music. On a deeper level, however, there is an immunological paranoia that such a forbiddingly esoteric practice has evidentially not died an immediate and natural death – one of a most barren poverty – but in fact amassed an international following even after its ideological annihilation by Adorno. Such a fact threatens to cede the hard-won subject positions of dodecaphonic historicism to conniving usurpers: Henze and Wildberger had been programmed alongside Goeyvaerts and Stockhausen, respectively, in the 1952 courses. This, then, is the 'change' that Rodemann is so eager to repudiate. His report is not merely dismissive, it is defensive. Of course, such categorical journalistic hostility recalls the reaction to Leibowitz's own entry at the Ferienkurse just four years

---

[113] 'Ja, und zwar mit Orchester', as Goeyvaerts has it; see ibid.   [114] Ibid.

[115] Albert Rodemann, 'Ein Tag des Experimentes: Zwei Veranstaltungen in den Kranichsteiner Ferienkursen', *Darmstädter Tagblatt,* 23 July 1952. Quoted and translated in Iddon, *New Music at Darmstadt,* 84–5.

prior. However, while critics were quick to note the umbilical connection between Leibowitz and his followers, the music of the 'younger generation' of the 1952 courses is described as a more autochthonous phenomenon. While clearly leery of Goeyvaerts's 'sect', Rodemann nevertheless posits a broader conceptual unity centred on Luigi Nono, 'the father of the Kranichstein model of the young compositional generation', praising his 'bold and charged abstraction'.[116] Here again Rodemann's reading is representative: the *Aachener Nachrichten* similarly describes a unified 'punctual style, which leads back to Anton Webern, and which the young H. K. [*sic*] Stockhausen still handles clumsily in his *Kreuzspiel*', which 'has found its master in Luigi Nono'.[117] It is nevertheless surprising that this category of 'punctual music' was not applied to the other pieces on the same programme, especially since both were by composers who had a far more sustained engagement with dodeca- phonic procedures than either Stockhausen, Nono, or Maderna: Camillo Togni's *Omaggio a Bach* and Jacques Wildberger's Quartet. Yet such a stylistic con- nection between Nono and Stockhausen had been proposed publicly less than two months prior to the Wunderkonzert in the radio broadcast of *Kreuzspiel*. Indeed, it was precisely the spuriousness of this link between Nono's music and Stockhausen's that Goeyvaerts had commented on to his friend. A critical mass of recent analytical scholarship bears out the conclusion that Goeyvaerts attrib- uted to his brother-in-law: Nono was doing something categorically different from Stockhausen in his compositional practice.[118] But the press did not have recourse to any sustained analytical reading of this new 'punctual' music. They had recourse to programmes, lectures, and the radio – all of which were mediated by Herbert Eimert. This is not to suggest that Eimert had singlehand- edly primed the press response to Darmstadt – if he had, surely more of them would have got Stockhausen's name correct – rather that nearly all available information on this music and the discourse which made sense of it would have been made available through him.

Correspondingly, while it is certain that the experience of the Wunderkonzert had made a strong impression on critics, their published responses suggest that this was typically a generalised and rather nebulous one. Iddon's study makes

---

[116] Ibid., 87.

[117] 'Die "Neue Musik" und die Gesellschaft: Für wen den eigentlich schaffen unsere Jüngsten?', *Aachener Nachrichten*, 25 July 1952. Quoted and translated in Iddon, *New Music at Darmstadt*, 87.

[118] See Iddon, *New Music at Darmstadt*, and 'Serial Canon(s): Nono's Variations and Boulez's Structures', *Contemporary Music Review*, 29.3 (2010), 265–75; compare also Sabbe, 'Einheit', with Veniero Rizzardi, 'The Tone Row, Squared: Bruno Maderna and the Birth of Serial Music in Italy', in *Rewriting Recent Music History: The Development of Early Serialism 1947–1957*, ed. Mark Delaere (Leuven: Peeters, 2011), 45–65.

much of the confusions, elisions, and erroneous recollections this concert produced in its wake. In a review which 'seemed to be making some reference to what Rodemann had said', the correspondent of the *Abendpost* complained that 'most of what was on offer in Kranichstein left the listener cold'. One might easily make the mistake of thinking that this remark referred to the Orff and Honegger operas or Strobel's Stravinsky hexalogy if the review did not immediately clarify the exact site of this coldness: 'The twelve-tone row has become a fetish and its propositions have become empty phrases. As justification, the pseudo-geniuses present their scores and point to interesting graphic images of their musical algorithms.'[119] Clearly, an extremely small number of performances of 'punctual music' almost completely dominated the critical discourse, to the extent that the title of Hille Moldenhauer's review deployed this zygotic repertoire as a metonym for the entirety of the courses: '"Punctual" Music and Indoor Slippers: Impressions of the International Courses for New Music'.[120] At this stage, Moldenhauer's impressions should be rather predictable: '"Punctual Music" is the shibboleth for this skeleton, whose secrets only its composers know'.[121] As Iddon is quick to note, such impressions of scientistic and obfuscatory composers did not seem to have a solid referent, and 'the only concrete event to which reference can have been being made was the session on electronic music and musique concrète on 21 July'[122] – the same day as the Wunderkonzert – which opened with lectures by Eimert and Werner Meyer-Eppler and concluded with Boulez's commentary on pieces of *musique concrète* by Schaeffer, Messiaen (*Timbres-durées*), and himself.[123] Eimert's lecture clearly had acted as something of a discursive will-o'-the-wisp for the Darmstadt press, with Walter Friedländer recapitulating a slightly garbled version of Eimert's historicist talking points in an effort to explain 'what was on offer this year in Darmstadt': '"Punctual" music is directly historically derived from twelve-tone music ... Even the next resultant step from "punctual" music can be inferred: electronic music.'[124] More surprisingly, just one week after the performance, Paul Müller's review for the *Rheinische Post* claims not only that Boulez was on the same programme as Stockhausen,

---

[119] Iddon, *New Music at Darmstadt*, 85.

[120] Hille Moldenhauer, '"Punktuelle" Musik und Filzpantoffeln: Eindrücke von den Internationalen Ferienkursen für Neue Musik', *Hamburger Echo*, 26 July 1952.

[121] Quoted and translated in Iddon, *New Music at Darmstadt*, 88.   [122] Ibid.

[123] See *Im Zenit der Moderne*, III.555.

[124] '"Punktuelle" Musik ist historisch unmittelbar aus der Zwölftonmusik abzuleiten ... Historisch ableitbar ist sogar noch die nächste aus der "punktuellen" Musik sich ergebende Stufe: die elektronische Musik.' Walter Friedländer, 'An den Grenzen der Hörbarkeit: Internationale Ferienkurse für Neue Musik in Darmstadt', *Der Standpunkt*, 8 August 1952; excerpted in Karl H. Wörner, *Karlheinz Stockhausen: Werk + Wollen, 1950–1962* (Rodenkirchen: P. J. Tonger, 1963), 126. This section is omitted in the English translation.

Nono, and Maderna, but that it was three *Structures* which were performed rather than the Second Piano Sonata.[125] In a retrospective essay published posthumously in the 1962 *Darmstädter Beiträge zur neuen Musik*, Steinecke himself capitalised on Müller's mistake, and gives the example of this imagined Wunderkonzert featuring Stockhausen, Maderna, Nono, and Boulez's *Structures* as an example of the varied stylistic orientations of the Darmstadt School in 1952.[126] On a more forthright note, Friedländer confessed that 'Karl Heinz [*sic*] Stockhausen's *Kreuzspiel* for chamber ensemble and Renzo dall'Oglio's *Cinque espressioni* for orchestra, both written in the "punctual" manner, can hardly be distinguished from one another.'[127] Such confusion is precisely the point, however. These muddled reports can only be mapped onto the literal events of the courses – the programmed concerts, workshops, and lectures – with extreme difficulty and circumspection, but match effortlessly onto the conceptual blueprint of New Music developed by Eimert and Steinecke. Iddon's conclusion that such historical revisionism 'enabled Steinecke quite literally to backdate the idea of the "Darmstadt School"' must therefore be gently qualified. Steinecke's conflation enacts the concept of a Darmstadt School which had been proposed by Eimert in early 1952 as a coherent, international movement capitalising on the untapped technical possibilities of Anton Webern's serial method. The creation of the Darmstadt School preceded its students and their practices.

If the press response to the 1952 courses may be seen to represent both a paradigmatic reversal in the discourse of post-war New Music and a definitive close to the primeval institutional history of Darmstadt, it is worthwhile to note that this reversal is fundamentally discursive. And as the press reports make clear, this reconciliation and its discursive stability is conditional on the young composers' willingness to play along. Here Nono's enthusiasm and sense of camaraderie carries the day: as a figure with reliable dodecaphonic credentials (his appearance at the 1950 courses having already resulted in his inclusion, with Maderna, in the grouping of 'young Italian dodecaphonists'),[128] Nono's adoption of Eimert's theoretical frame at the beginning of 1952 ensured the conceptual unity of this emergent Darmstadt School in the discourse surrounding the courses. Thus

---

[125] Paul Müller, 'Schmelztiegel der Neuen Musik: Abschluß der Kranichstein Tage', *Rheinische Post*, 30 July 1952; cited in Iddon, *New Music at Darmstadt*, 83.

[126] Wolfgang Steinecke, 'Kranichstein – Geschichte, Idee, Ergebnisse', *Darmstädter Beiträge zur neuen Musik*, 4 (1962), 9–24.

[127] Walter Friedländer, 'An den Grenzen der Hörbarkeit: Internationale Ferienkurse für Neue Musik in Darmstadt', *Der Standpunkt*, 8 August 1952; quoted in Iddon, *New Music at Darmstadt*, 86.

[128] Walter Harth, 'Musik-Olympiade der Jüngsten', *Der Kurier*, 8 September 1950; cited in Iddon, *New Music at Darmstadt*, 38–9.

Goeyvaerts and Stockhausen's barren cultic practice is rejected on its own terms; but as an extreme morphological variant of the spirit of the younger generation, more healthily exhibited in Nono, it is conditionally – and grudgingly – accepted as New Music. It remained to be seen, however, whether Goeyvaerts and Stockhausen would themselves accept their position within the Darmstadt School.

4 Stability and Its Consequences

4.1 Goeyvaerts

After sending a light-hearted letter from Antwerp detailing his return, dated 28 July 1952 and ending with a request for his friend to 'write me a long letter',[129] Goeyvaerts's correspondence with Stockhausen breaks off for more than three months. Occupied only with the completion of *Nummer 4 met dode tonen* (1952) and freelance jobs (including a stint as a replacement organist),[130] Goeyvaerts's sense of alienation was exacerbated. Recalling this post-Darmstadt slump in his memoirs, Goeyvaerts writes: 'One thing became very clear to me as a result of all that had happened: I was facing a period of prolonged loneliness.'[131] *Opus 2* and *Opus 3 met gestreken en geslagen tonen* were performed in Belgium, and if any interest was generated by them, neither Goeyvaerts nor the press make any note of it. The performance of *Opus 3* at the 1953 ISCM World Music Days in Oslo, on the other hand, did generate mild attention, all of it negative. Edward Clark's review in *The Musical Times* is illustrative here. After a rhetorically posed introduction ('What of the younger men? It is to these that one instinctively looks for indications of new developments'), Clark immediately concludes that '[t]he exponents of "experimental" techniques failed to convince on this occasion'.[132] The two 'exponents' Clark cites are Goeyvaerts and Milton Babbitt. The latter's song cycle, Clark determines, 'failed' on expressionistic grounds, 'because he did not follow Schönberg, who once explained to the writer that a composer chose words to set which enabled his music to express itself, not the other way round'.[133] Goeyvaerts's failure, fittingly, is rather more absolute:

> The piece by Karel Goeyvaerts 'aux sons frappes et frottés' [*sic*] was a disappointment to listeners familiar with the compositions of Edgard Varèse, Darius Milhaud and others or with the fascinating examples of 'musique concrète' recently heard in various countries. Particularly unconvincing was the use of stringed instruments, violins and cellos, only to produce single notes. The effect of the whole was static.[134]

---

[129] Goeyvaerts to Stockhausen, 28 July 1952; *Selbstlose Musik*, 332–3.   [130] Ibid.
[131] Goeyvaerts, 'Paris – Darmstadt', 50.
[132] Edward Clark, 'The I. S. C. M. Festival', *The Musical Times*, 94.1326 (1953), 377–8.
[133] Ibid., 377.   [134] Ibid.

Clark's perspective here is reminiscent of Eimert's two years prior at the 1951 Darmstadt courses, when he played Goeyvaerts's *Tre lieder* to illustrate the maximalist strains of Parisian instrumental music and its kinship with Varèse. And it was as a pupil of Milhaud that Goeyvaerts first made his name – and the acquaintance of Eimert – with this same piece at the 1950 ISCM festival. Clark's 'disappointment', then, is not only understandable, it is remarkably perceptive: if Goeyvaerts was the same composer, with the same aesthetic practice, as he had been in 1950, then the timbral reduction to only the eponymous 'bowed and struck tones' (the former furthermore played *sempre senza vibrato*) made little sense. Ironically, however, Clark's final comment suggests that the music did precisely what Goeyvaerts wanted it to do, although Clark clearly reads this 'static' effect as a negative outcome. It is Clark's remove from the post-Webernian conversation which allows him to give one of the most aesthetically coherent readings of Goeyvaerts's music at this time, as a static disappointment of dynamic expectations. Without the tethers of 'punctual music', 'post-Webernianism', or the Darmstadt School, *Opus 3* was experienced as a misfire, unconnected with more fruitful 'experiments'. Left outside the hothouse of the newly christened Darmstadt School, Goeyvaerts's practice withered.

Clark's account appears to coincide with a BBC review of the festival Goeyvaerts remembers for 'a series of derisory remarks about my text in the programme – a text which they had not understood at all'.[135] A letter from Goeyvaerts to Stockhausen mentions that 'lots of commotion and laughter' were audible in the live broadcast, suggesting that the commentators were not the only ones left in bewilderment.[136] Such misunderstandings had concrete professional ramifications for the young composer – no doubt further contributing to his sense of marginalisation – and Goeyvaerts's professional contacts in the Francosphere seemed to abruptly dry up since he had relocated to his home country. After his circuitous return from Darmstadt in late July 1952, Goeyvaerts became interested in the possibilities of electronically generated sound, particularly 'sinus tones', drafting *Nummer 4 met dode tonen* in the winter of 1952, which, as Sabbe notes, is most likely the first work intended to be realised through purely electronic means.[137] Eager to pursue this work, Goeyvaerts

---

[135] Goeyvaerts, 'Paris – Darmstadt', 50.

[136] Goeyvaerts to Stockhausen, 18 July 1953; *Selbstlose Musik*, 352.

[137] Sabbe, 'K. Goeyvaerts', 70. Sabbe's defence of the piece, though spirited, likely does more harm than good for any reader interested in a re-evaluation of Goeyvaerts's position in New Music historiography (which is, after all, Sabbe's explicit purpose here). From his description of the work ('may be the most radical pretension to totality and positivism ever presented in aesthetic terms') to the positive comparison to Babbitt's most infamous tract, Sabbe is clearly attempting here, as elsewhere, to accommodate Goeyvaerts within a historical discourse and teleology which flatly has no place for him or his practice.

petitioned the critic and musicologist Paul Collaer, who had previously been instrumental in securing performances of his music in Paris and was now the head of the NIR, to be granted permission to experiment with sinus tones on equipment available in the studio. The request was 'flatly refused' by Collaer.[138] This rejection clearly stung, since Goeyvaerts's memoir takes time to mention that 'a few years later, I bumped into Collaer at a concert [and] he spoke with admiration of the *Gesang der Jünglinge*, the first fully home-grown product of the Cologne Studio. He probably no longer thought of the chance he had missed two years earlier.'[139] Goeyvaerts has somewhat muddled the chronology in this recollection: his request to work with sine waves was rejected in 1953, and *Gesang der Jünglinge* was not performed until 1956, so the chance Collaer had missed in fact occurred at least *three* years before this conversation happened. It is tempting to read this error as confirmation that Collaer's rejection was still fresh in Goeyvaerts's mind, as the aside is among the most uncharacteristically embittered that Goeyvaerts makes in his entire autobiography.

Goeyvaerts chalks up Collaer's neglect to the fact that Goeyvaerts no longer moved in Francophone circles, writing that Collaer 'had suddenly become cooler in my regard since I had left Milhaud and gone back to my native country to try and pursue a career. It went so far that my compositions, hitherto accepted for performance virtually as a matter of course, now ended up at the bottom of some drawer and were forgotten.'[140] As it happens, Collaer had not forgotten about Goeyvaerts at all: an index in his 1955 book *La Musique moderne* lists Goeyvaerts's *Tre Lieder per sonare a venti-sei*, the same piece he had enthusiastically broadcast half a decade prior, as one of the seven most important compositions of 1949, alongside Schoenberg's *A Survivor from Warsaw* and Britten's *Spring Symphony*.[141] Indeed, Goeyvaerts is one of only nine composers born after 1920 who are mentioned in the book.[142] In the text itself, however, Collaer's enthusiasm for Goeyvaerts is more measured. He is initially mentioned alongside Stockhausen as one of the two most representative examples of 'analytical' trends in young composers.[143] Collaer's opinion of such trends can be gleaned from a later description, no doubt informed by Goeyvaerts's abortive request to him in 1953: 'Karel Goeyvaerts, shaped by Messiaen and Milhaud, has renounced all other forms of composition to express

---

[138] Goeyvaerts, 'Paris – Darmstadt', 48.　　[139] Ibid.　　[140] Ibid., 47.

[141] Paul Collaer, *La Musique Moderne: 1905–1955* (Paris: Elsevier, 1955), 21.

[142] Ibid., 24. The other eight are Bruno Maderna (1920), Lukas Foss (1922), Maurice Le Roux (1923), Pierre Boulez (1925), Gieselher Klebe (1925), Hans Werner Henze (1926), Luigi Nono (1926), and Karlheinz Stockhausen (1928).

[143] '. . . des musiciens tels que Karlheinz Stockhausen et Karel Goeyvaerts sont jusqu'à présent les plus représentatifs d'une periode à peine amorcée qui e n'est encore à sa phase analytique'. Ibid., 26.

himself exclusively with electronic music.'[144] It would appear, then, that Collaer's neglect stemmed far more from discursive considerations than geographical or nationalist ones. What is more, these apprehensions echo those voiced earlier by Clark, emplotting Goeyvaerts as a promising composer from a solid background who had gone off the deep end. Like Hauer, he had all the trappings of New Music while remaining fundamentally outside of its evolution.

Still, Goeyvaerts's hopes for both a broader understanding of his musical practice and a sympathetic institutional setting for him to pursue his increasingly abstracted ideal of 'static music' – which now had become so ascetic that only electronically generated tones could be permitted – were not totally extinguished. He approached Vic Legley, who was engaged to conduct a concert with *Kreuzspiel, Opus 3*, and Nono's *Polifonica – Monodica – Ritmica* on 14 April 1953 which would subsequently be broadcast, in an attempt to find support in realising *Nummer 4* in the studio. Although Goeyvaerts later recalls that Legley was 'unable to understand why I wanted to use sinus tones in my compositions',[145] a letter to Stockhausen from 20 February 1953 describes Legley as 'very interested' in *Nummer 4*, and he 'immediately' put Goeyvaerts in touch with laboratory technicians at the NIR.[146] However, this too ended briskly in disappointment, resulting in tones that were 'certainly not dead, and in fact more alive than, say, a clarinet tone'.[147]

4.2 Stockhausen

In November 1952, Goeyvaerts resumed his correspondence with Stockhausen in an enthusiastic letter detailing the composition of *Nummer 4* and his hopes for working with electronically generated sound in a studio environment.[148] Stockhausen very much shared these hopes. Both inspired and disappointed in the work Boulez and Barraqué had been doing under Schaeffer, Stockhausen had repeatedly written to Eimert throughout 1952 encouraging him to create a studio for compositional experiments with purely electronically generated sounds.[149] Not long after Goeyvaerts had written this letter, Eimert wrote to Stockhausen that the intendant of the NWDR had advised Stockhausen that 'you should duly complete your studies in Paris and afterwards take on no

---

[144] ' ... Karel Goeyvaerts, formé par Messiaen et Milhaud, et qui renonce à toute autre forme de composition pour s'exprimer uniquement par la musique électronique'. Ibid., 289.

[145] Goevyaerts, 'Paris – Darmstadt', 47.

[146] Goeyvaerts to Stockhausen, 20 February 1953; *Selbstlose Musik*, 341–2.

[147] Goeyvaerts to Stockhausen, 14 March 1953; *Selbstlose Musik*, 343.

[148] Goeyvaerts to Stockhausen, 12 November 1952; *Selbstlose Musik*, 333–4.

[149] See especially Stockhausen to Eimert, 20 March 1952; Kirchmeyer, 'Elektronische Messe', 242–5.

further work without consulting with us'.[150] Eimert suggested that a one-year contract would be arranged for Stockhausen and 'other close collaborators' on his return to Cologne, characterising this development as 'a stroke of fate'.[151]

Alongside this good news, Eimert describes the vast possibilities afforded by the studio's technology, with which 'one can organise all imaginable sounds', suggesting that electronically generated sound can radically expand or replace, for example, 'the available material of the violin developed in the epoch from Corelli to Brahms' with 'a certain musical total-principle' or 'a pure application principle' which would reconfigure the fundamentals of sound in a manner far exceeding 'the limits of playability'.[152] In view of such opportunities, Eimert suggests that Stockhausen might rethink his current practice: 'With these considerations, I would like to encourage you to also be on the lookout for other formal principles.'[153] In case the implication here is too subtle, Eimert turns to a concrete example in a broadcast of Stockhausen's *Spiel* he had listened to 11 December, in which it seemed to him that Stockhausen's present compositional methods had reached the limits of their effectiveness. '[W]ith such highly organised "Point Music"', Eimert warns, in characteristically technical language, 'the production and decay processes of the instruments are very essential – if one removes them, and this indeed is what happens with barbaric tape-editing, then something mechanical rolls along, like in the rhythmic tape studies of Messiaen and Boulez', contrasting such a 'sequence of blind sounds' with 'the tremendous vividness of electronic music'.[154] As it happened, Goeyvaerts had also listened to the 11 December broadcast of *Spiel*, and was far more appreciative in his response to his younger friend: 'For the first time it has emphatically struck me that this music actually avails "selfless being". Where almost all music takes the listener to some state of excitement, here one experiences just the opposite: a great peace, in which one barely thinks or feels.'[155] It is precisely the undifferentiated, static unfolding that concerned Eimert which Goeyvaerts takes as Stockhausen's ultimate mastery of his art.

---

[150] Eimert to Stockhausen, 8 December 1952; 'Elektronische Messe', 247–8. Eimert must have intimated something along these lines to Stockhausen previously, since Goeyvaerts's letter of 5 December begins with congratulating Stockhausen on 'good news' received from Eimert (see *Selbstlose Musik*, 335).

[151] Eimert to Stockhausen, 8 December 1952; Kirchmeyer, 'Elektronische Messe,' 248.

[152] Ibid.

[153] 'Mit solchen Überlegungen möchte ich Sie anregen, auch noch nach andern Gestaltungsprinzipien Ausschau zu halten.' Ibid.

[154] Ibid.

[155] 'Zum ersten Mal ist es mir besonders aufgefallen, dass diese Musik wirklich zum "selbstlosen Sein" hilft. Wo fast alle Musik den Zuhörer in irgendeinen Zustand von Aufregung bringt, empfindet man hier gerade das Gegenteil: Eine große Ruhe, bei der man kaum noch denkt und fühlt.' Goeyvaerts to Stockhausen, 12 December 1952; *Selbstlose Musik*, 337.

'Punctual' or otherwise, Stockhausen was under increasing pressure to alter the compositional practice that he had developed from Goeyvaerts and Messiaen. Eimert's reservations resonate with Boulez's negative reactions to Goeyvaerts during his stay in Paris. Doubtless Stockhausen had initially brushed these off – his letters to Eimert during his time in Paris are uniformly enthusiastic about Goeyvaerts, and he even mentions that Boulez 'cannot make much of Goeyvaerts' simply because the Belgian 'is ahead of us all'.[156] But Boulez was clearly threatened: Peyser's biography mentions an unspecified later event in which Stockhausen was 'trying to undermine Boulez' by pointing out that Goeyvaerts's Sonata for Two Pianos had been composed before the first book of *Structures*.[157] Boulez's response, as reported by Peyser, clearly reveals what is at stake: 'Goeyvaerts is an invention of Stockhausen's. He was to me what Hauer was to Schoenberg.'[158] Again, Goeyvaerts is placed definitively outside the discourse of New Music. As such, Stockhausen's position must be re-evaluated. In Peyser's telling, Stockhausen had simply been 'young and awed by Goeyvaerts', but lost his naivety as soon as he met Boulez:

> Immediately, under the influence of the slightly older and immensely power-ful man, Stockhausen made the shift from Schoenberg to Webern and to an extension of the serial principle to areas other than pitch relations. Within a year Stockhausen returned to Cologne and the post-Webern movement took roots in Germany.[159]

While, as Kovács has noted, Peyser's credentials as a music historian are not uncontested (it appears she may herself have been 'under the influence of the slightly older and immensely powerful man'), her narrative here is an unmis-takable emplotment from Anglophone historiography. It is for this reason that Peyser can immediately assure her readers that 'Boulez's depreciation of Goeyvaerts's talent is echoed by other specialists in the field' – Boulez, like Schoenberg, is the important composer; Goeyvaerts, like Hauer, is an esoteric eccentric. Boulez and Schoenberg are the centre; Goeyvaerts and Hauer are the periphery. Yet this emplotment is confused even on its own terms: if Stockhausen was under the influence of Goeyvaerts, how could Boulez have introduced him to techniques he already knew?

Stockhausen certainly seems to be a peculiarly contested commodity. In his 'small monograph' on Eimert, Helmut Kirchmeyer credits the older composer and theorist not only with the 'discovery' of Stockhausen but very nearly his de facto adoption:

---

[156] Stockhausen to Eimert, 10 March 1952; Kirchmeyer, 'Elektronische Messe', 241.
[157] Joan Peyser, *Boulez: Conductor, Composer, Enigma* (London: Cassell, 1976), 77.
[158] Ibid.   [159] Ibid.

The Eimert–Stockhausen relationship was as tight as it could possibly be between two men of such an age difference. Stockhausen no longer had any parents. His father had disappeared on the Hungarian front, his mother was murdered by the National Socialists in Cologne. The Eimerts' marriage remained childless. For Eimert, Stockhausen became a son for whom he would do everything. He advised him, recommended Paris as a place of study, sent him to Darmstadt for the New Music Courses, drummed up his first commissions and, with great effort, brought him into the electronic studio as a semi-permanent artistic collaborator in 1953.[160]

If the implication was not clear enough here, Kirchmeyer later makes it explicit: 'Stockhausen was Eimert's follower.'[161] And, of course, there is always Herman Sabbe, who has asserted that Stockhausen's work instead 'followed in the footsteps' of Goeyvaerts in numerous publications over the course of almost half a century.[162] What is at issue here is not which one of these accounts is more truthful than the others, but rather the terms on which they establish their truth claim over the person and music of Karlheinz Stockhausen.

Despite Stockhausen's Damascene initiation into the Messiaen–Goeyvaerts–Barraqué tradition, which radically transformed his compositional practice – a *Stunde Null* if there ever was one – in retrospect, at least, Stockhausen appeared unready to acknowledge a 'mature style' either in *Kreuzspiel* or subsequent works like *Spiel*, *Schlagtrio*, and *Punkte*. At the time, however, Stockhausen seemed far more confident of having reached compositional maturity. Adopting Goeyvaerts's rather austere *Nummer*-system, he designated *Kreuzspiel* as Nr. 1, *Spiel* as Nr. 2, *Schlagtrio* (formerly *Schlagquartett*) as Nr. 3, and *Punkte* as Nr. 4.[163] After the Donaueschingen premiere of an abridged version of *Punkte* on 11 October 1952, Stockhausen was introduced to Alfred Schlee, the head of Universal Edition, who expressed interest in publishing his music. While he did sign a contract with Universal – and continued to correspond with Schlee, who, in early 1953, promised to send Stockhausen all of Webern's published scores in preparation for a 'Webern evening' Eimert was

---

[160] 'Das Verhältnis Eimert-Stockhausen wurde so eng, wie es zwischen Männern solchen Altersunterschieds überhaupt werden konnte. Stockhausen hatte keine Eltern mehr. Der Vater war während des Krieges an der ungarischen Front verschollen, die Mutter war von den Nationalsozialisten in Köln ermordet worden. Die Ehe Eimerts blieb kinderlos. Stockhausen wurde für Eimert zum Sohn, für den er alles tat. Er beriet ihn, empfahl ihm Paris als Studienort, schickte ihn nach Darmstadt zu den Kursen neuer Musik, verschaffte ihm die ersten Kompositionsaufträge und holte ihn 1953 unter großen Mühen als halbfesten künstlerischen Mitarbeiter in das elektronische Studio.' Kirchmeyer, *Kleine Monographie*, 9.

[161] 'Stockhausen wurde Eimerts Nachfolger.' Ibid., 13.

[162] The source of this particular phrasing is Sabbe, 'The New Music in the 20th Century – a Number of Key Concepts Essential for Interpretation', in *Inter Disciplinas Ars*, ed. Peter Dejans (Leuven: Leuven University Press, 1998), 84.

[163] See Christoph von Blumröder, *Die Grundlegung der Musik Karlheinz Stockhausens* (Stuttgart: Franz Steiner, 1993), 99 (fn. 86).

planning for that year's Darmstadt courses – Stockhausen did not opt to publish any music with Universal at this point. Stockhausen's next composition, which began with the readily Goeyvaertsian title of *Nr. 5 für 10 Instrumente*, clearly took on a more epochal significance for the composer, who changed the title later to *Kontrapunkte* and *Nr. 1 für 10 Instrumente*, before finally splitting the difference in *Kontra-Punkte* with the designation Nr. 1.[164]

As Nr. 1, *Kontra-Punkte* became Stockhausen's first commercially published score,[165] concomitant with an overhaul of his official *Werkverzeichnis*: *Kreuzspiel* was now merely Nr. 1/7, the first in a series leading up, via Nr. 1/2, *Punkte*, to *Kontra-Punkte*.[166] Clearly, this was a new(er) beginning for Stockhausen's *oeuvre*. In a short commentary appended to the score, Stockhausen describes the work in a starkly technical vocabulary as a juxtaposition of 'the dimensions of sound, also known as "parameters"; this happens in a prescribed fourdimensional [*sic*] space: lengths (durations), heights (frequencies), volume (loudnesses [*sic*]) and forms of vibration (timbres)'.[167] Yet the metaphysical concerns familiar from *Kreuzspiel* are not totally absent: Stockhausen's note concludes with a description of 'an unique and extremely unified contruction [*sic*]. A hidden force which creates cohesion; related proportions: a structure. Not the same figures in a changing light. Rather this: different figures in the same, all-penetrating light.'[168]

Nevertheless, it was the parameters rather than the all-penetrating light which became emblematic of the Darmstadt School's increasingly secure presence in the discourse of New Music. Whether the pressure was more from Boulez or from Eimert, Stockhausen now described his practice with reference to a toolkit of advanced techniques rather than a cipher-play – a *Glasperlenspiel* – of some kind of extra-temporal truth. The vocabulary from the foreword to the score of *Kontra-Punkte* is repeated nearly verbatim in Stockhausen's contribution to the Webern symposium organised by Eimert on 23 July 1953 in Darmstadt and later broadcast on the NWDR *Nachtprogramme* presented by Eimert on 12 November of the

---

[164] Ibid., 99–101; Blumröder also mentions 'KONTRA-PUNKTEN', but this appears to just be a typo.

[165] UE (Universal Edition) 12 207.

[166] See Blumröder, *Grundlegung*, 79; Stockhausen retained this numbering system for the rest of his life, although it is not commonly used as a reference even within the Stockhausen-Verlag, and the numbering seems distinctly unhelpful in distinguishing between the nested, modular scenes of *LICHT*. At present, Stockhausen's *oeuvre* is organised from Nr. 1/11, *Chöre für Doris*, to Nr. 101, *PARADIES*, the '21st hour' of *KLANG*. See the worklist available in English and German from the Stockhausen-Verlag, available in English at www.karlheinzstockhausen.org /pdf/Karlheinz_Stockhausen_Works_English.pdf (accessed 30.8.2019).

[167] See *Kontra-Punkte*, UE 12 207 (Universal Edition: 1953). The English translation given in the score, which is retained here, makes Stockhausen's description even more obtusely technical: *Höhen*, which clearly has the implication of *Tonhöhen* (pitches), is translated as 'heights'; similarly, *Lautstärke* would more intuitively be rendered 'dynamics' rather than 'loudnesses'.

[168] Ibid.

same year. Here, Stockhausen credits 'Webern's approach to the new compositional principles' as postulating a 'functional connection' between 'all three dimensions of the acoustic world', which he defines as 'relationships between time-durations, pitches and dynamics [*Zeitdauern, Tonhöhen und Lautstärken*]'.[169] In self-imposed exile (or, at least, self-justified non-presence) from Darmstadt, Goeyvaerts sent his contribution to the Webern evening in a letter to Stockhausen.[170] In this piece, entitled 'Anton Webern, Departure Point of an Evolution', Goeyvaerts frames his argument as Stockhausen has, by claiming that 'Webern is distinguished from Schoenberg and all other twelve-tone composers' through his 'application of sound material as a medium for the realisation of a structural network'.[171] However, Goeyvaerts immediately emphasises the 'spiritual foundation' of such a method, since 'not a person, but a way of being should govern the tones. Music becomes an image of an essence, the composer becomes an artificer of the tones.'[172]

For his part, Eimert presented these two short expositions, alongside contributions from Nono and Boulez, as representing not only a unified compositional methodology but a proscriptive aesthetic program for New Music. Much of Eimert's argument had not been altered from his 'limit-situation' lecture with Steinecke two years prior: he again presents Webern's music as 'having thought through the twelve-tone system until its final abstracted territory, behind which silence appears to stand', which nevertheless signifies 'that this supposed end of music is at once a beginning'.[173] As Eimert continues, however, the thrust of his argument immediately becomes far more direct than it was in 1951: 'a beginning, in any case, for a group of young composers, who do not let the latest fashionable slogan, the "musical humanity" *("musikalischen Humanitas"*), go unchallenged, and with unshakeable faith and strength of belief see in Webern the definitive master of the totality of New Music'.[174]

For one familiar with English-language historiography of New Music, this formulation is far from unexpected, and nicely encapsulates an idea put rather more disparagingly by Richard Taruskin – that post-war European serialism was little more than a manifestation of 'the desperate antihumanism [*sic*] of the early atomic age'.[175] While it may be contested that Eimert does not seem to come across as particularly desperate either here or elsewhere, it is hard to

---

[169] See Eimert, 'Junge Komponisten bekennen sich zu Anton Webern', in *Im Zenit der Moderne*, III.64.

[170] Goeyvaerts to Stockhausen, 18 July 1953; *Selbstlose Musik*, 352. Stockhausen prepared a typescript from this, reproduced in *Im Zenit der Moderne*, III.61–2 (fn. 1), gently editing, clarifying, and tightening up Goeyvaerts's German (e.g. 'geistigen Grundlagen' becomes 'Geistesgrund').

[171] Goeyvaerts, 'Anton Webern, Ausgangspunkt einer Evolution', in *Selbstlose Musik*, 138.

[172] Ibid.   [173] Ibid., III.58.   [174] Ibid.

[175] Taruskin, *Music in the Late Twentieth Century, The Oxford History of Western Music*, V (Oxford: Oxford University Press, 2005), 43.

dispute that, for whatever reason, he has placed the Darmstadt School as his avatar against what might very well be read as the humanistic impulse *in toto*. [176] Nevertheless, in the context of the present study, such a formulation should appear rather bizarre, not least since Goeyvaerts and Nono had repeatedly and publicly emphasised their desire for their music to inculcate some sort of new, quasi-utopian community. [177] Indeed, if any such commonality might be demonstrated between the members of the Darmstadt School as it stood in 1953 – Goeyvaerts, Stockhausen, Boulez, Nono, Maderna – it may very well be made fruitfully on terms precisely inverse to Eimert's proposal, from a shared concern with a new, more integral relationship between composer, music, and public (and, for Goeyvaerts and Stockhausen, God). Eimert himself certainly was aware that there was little to justify this characterisation, but nevertheless maintains its enunciative coherency. Such a paradoxical position is clear from his letter to Steinecke describing the Webern symposium at Darmstadt, which at once presents Eimert as the transparent advocate of the Darmstadt School and expresses bemused mockery at Nono's straying from the script:

> I thought that I would start off and, for a couple of minutes, present the general situation from the perspective of the young composers. Then Nono would say something about the hu-uman [*das Määnschlich*] for 5 to 6 minutes, followed by Stockhausen talking shop for ca. 15 minutes. [178]

Indeed, Nono himself had written to Steinecke three days prior, expressing an explicit desire, as it were, to rescue Webern from advocates like Eimert: '[I want to] say something new about Webern, against the mentality for which Webern is practically just high-abstract mathematics, and against those who speak of his music only with formulas.' [179] For Eimert, Goeyvaerts was even further from the mark, and, unlike Nono, Boulez, and probably Stockhausen, Goeyvaerts was asked to provide an alternative essay for the subsequent *Nachtprogramm* broadcast. [180] This second essay, given the rather less equivocal title 'Perpetual Renewal of Music: Avowal to Anton Webern', maintains the overall course of Goeyvaerts's earlier argument – Webern is differentiated from

---

[176] A further investigation, either discursive, aesthetic, or psychological, into potential causes for this evident 'antihumanism' would unfortunately risk completely engorging the already distended biographical exegesis of Eimert in the present study.

[177] Most succinctly, in Goeyvaerts's programme note to the 1952 Darmstadt performance of his Second Violin Concerto.

[178] Eimert to Steinecke, 22 June 1953; quoted and translated in Carola Nielinger-Vakil, *Luigi Nono: A Composer in Context* (Cambridge: Cambridge University Press, 2015), fn. 123. It is most likely not coincidental that Stockhausen's talk was allotted thrice the time of Nono's.

[179] Nono to Steinecke, 19 June 1953; quoted in Borio, 'Kontinuität der Moderne?', *Im Zenit der Moderne*, I.216.

[180] See *Im Zenit der Moderne*, III.61 (fn. 1).

'twelve-tone music from Schoenberg to Dallapiccola' by his structural innovations – but replaces reference to 'spiritual foundations' with the more amenably Eimertian concept of 'parallel technical and physical findings', and presents metahistorical phenomena which prefigure Webern's practice, such as 'the splintering of tonality after *Tristan*' and 'the decomposition of rhythm in Stravinsky's *Sacre*'.[181] Writing to Henri Pousseur, Goeyvaerts seems upset at Eimert's mediation of his writing, describing a hope that cultural gatekeepers who advocate for their music will 'be of good will', before admitting that such is not presently the case: 'It's the attitude we've adopted with Eimert and God knows he keeps spouting nonsense . . . '.[182] Here, once again, an almost absolute disjuncture is maintained between the structural discourse of New Music and its practice; its enunciation as a discourse effectively irreconcilable with – or, more pointedly, irrelevant to – the practices of its subjects. As such, Taruskin's claim re-establishes a discursive truth even though it cannot be applied to the music or thought of any of the composers it represents.

Irreconcilabilities aside, Eimert is far from finished. Teasing out the significance of this 'truly astonishing event', which has thrown 'the seemingly most esoteric musician from the Schoenberg circle suddenly into the centre' of the latest technical developments of music production, Eimert anticipates some objections which are almost eerily reminiscent of those voiced half a century later by Taruskin: 'A physical-mathematical music then? A "game of Mandarins", like Honegger once called it? Is it really? And furthermore it would be asked: here, in the wake of great physical upheavals, shall a musical materialism be reared which has forgotten the human origin of art?'[183] The source of such objections, Eimert suggests in no uncertain terms, is Theodor Adorno, prefigured in the language of centricity and esoterica: 'I betray no secret: the criticism on Webern today is essentially Adorno's criticism, subservient to Schoenbergian dialectics, which has designated the situation of these young composers as a "situation of the broken"', a verdict Eimert compares to the arguments of Hans Pfitzner during the 1930s.[184] Once again, this is a seemingly odd rhetorical move (although, in all fairness,

---

[181] Goeyvaerts, 'Ständige Erneuerung der Musik: Bekenntnis zu Anton Webern', in *Selbstlose Musik*, 140–1.

[182] 'C'est l'attitude que nous avons adopté avec Eimert et Dieu sait s'il dit encore des inepties . . . ' Goeyvaerts to Pousseur, 23 October 1953; *Selbstlose Musik*, 394–5.

[183] 'Eine physikalisch-mathematische Musik also? Eine "Spiel der Mandarine", wie Honegger es einmal nannte? Ist es wirklich so? Und weiter wäre zu fragen: wird hier im Gefolge der großen physikalischen Umwälzungen ein musikalischer Materialismus herangezüchtet, der den menschlichen Ursprung der Kunst vergessen hat?' Eimert, 'Junge Komponisten bekennen sich', *Im Zenit der Moderne*, III.58–9.

[184] 'Ich verrate kein Geheimnis: die Kritik an Webern ist heute im Wesentlichen die in der Schoenbergschen Dialektik befangene Kritik Adornos, der die Situation dieser jungen Komponisten als eine "Situation des Kaputt" bezeichnet hat.' Ibid, III.59.

Eimert's comparison between Pfitzner and Adorno on the basis of a sort of world-historical *Kulturpessimismus* is rather perceptive, judging from both men's admiration for the historiography of Oswald Spengler), positioning the most prominent theorist of New Music against the discursive formation he had himself developed. [185] Nevertheless, Eimert maintains that the 'young composers' are enacting precisely the teleological event envisioned by Adornian-Leibowitzian historicism; as Eimert puts it, 'the powerful lesson issued to us by the history of occidental music is that the musical material came and has come to address us on its own terms'. [186] The issue then, for Eimert, is not that the Adornian-Leibowitzian discourse of New Music was in error, but rather that its theorists were too blinkered to see its natural development from Webern to the 'young composers' of the Darmstadt School. Indeed, the sheer scope of his assembled advocates operates as Eimert's concluding QED: 'if these young composers – at the moment individuals in France, Italy, Belgium, Germany, Sweden, and the United States – if these young composers now learn again the material language identified from music, then they do so as people of the 20th century.' [187]

Such a turn from metaphysics to Webern was at once discursive, aesthetic, ideological, professional, and deeply personal. Goeyvaerts quickly became aware that his young friend was after something rather different in *Kontra-Punkte*; after hearing a radio broadcast of the piece that was 'very sensibly introduced' by a discussion between Eimert and Stockhausen in the summer of 1953, Goeyvaerts was struck by the incipient materialism of the music, writing to Stockhausen, 'as its first process, this music already has a conception of sound; you can't deny that'. [188] For Goeyvaerts, this is 'more than just a formal issue'; it represents a fundamental divergence in practice and understanding. In a subsequent letter, Goeyvaerts clarifies his view of this divergence: 'For me, sounds only come at the end, after the spiritual structure is so definite that nothing more may be changed.' [189] While Goeyvaerts still maintained that 'differences are necessary for love' in 1953, [190] his friendship with Stockhausen chilled over the next four years

---

[185] In 1950, Adorno had published the essay 'Spengler nach dem Untergang', which drew comparisons between Spengler's historical conclusions and Adorno's own, especially in *Dialektik der Aufklärung*. See Adorno, 'Spengler nach dem Untergang', *Der Monat*, 3.20 (1950), 115–28.

[186] Ibid.

[187] ' … wenn nun diese jungen Komponisten – vorerst noch einzelne in Frankreich, Italien, Belgien, Deutschland, Schweden und die Vereinigten Staaten – wenn diese Jungen nun die mit der Musik identische Materialsprache wieder erlernen, dann tun sie es als Menschen des 20. Jahrhundert.' Ibid.

[188] Goeyvaerts to Stockhausen, 18 July 1953; *Selbstlose Musik*, 352.

[189] 'Bei mir kommen die Klänge erst am Schluss, nachdem die geistige Struktur so definitiv ist, dass nichts mehr geändert werden kann.' Goeyvaerts to Stockhausen, 4 August 1953; *Selbstlose Musik*, 353.

[190] Goeyvaerts to Stockhausen, 18 July 1953; *Selbstlose Musik*, 352.

before breaking off definitively. On 24 September 1958, Goeyvaerts sent his final letter to Karlheinz and Doris, an invitation to his wedding.[191] They did not attend.[192]

4.3 New Music Reconciled

While the critics at Darmstadt seemed satisfied with Eimert's explanation for this newer New Music, Adorno was not quite as easily placated. But even at his most polemic, Adorno never seriously questioned that these pieces were, in fact, self-evidently New Music. Rather, what he questioned was the supposed falsely metaphysical content of these works, in largely identical terms to how he responded to Goeyvaerts and Stockhausen's performance at the 1951 courses. As such, Adorno's complaint against recent works of New Music, as articulated in *Das Altern der neuen Musik*, is not so much that the works of 'the iconoclastic exponents of "pointillist" music' are barren and atrophied (since, for Adorno, they axiomatically are), but rather that pointillist music as a practice has somehow abdicated (Adorno suggests repression) its capacity to understand its own historical-material-social condition. 'In them', Adorno writes of such pieces, 'meaninglessness becomes the program, though sometimes dressed up with Existentialism: in place of subjective intention, Being itself is supposed to be heard.'[193] But precisely because of the high degree of technical advancement which they employ – Adorno takes Eimert at his word here – 'this music is anything but that of primal sources; it is subjectively and historically mediated to the extreme'.[194] It is telling, too, that the Roman Catholic God is so far from Adorno's discourse that the closest concept he can reach for is 'primal sources'. Indeed, the recourse to 'Being' is itself quickly and rather incoherently elided with more comfortably Adornoian concepts like 'the rationalization of art' and 'the scientization of art', before finally becoming nothing more than a Freudian tic: 'Deluded, man sets up something artefactual as a primal phenomenon, and prays to it; an authentic instance of fetishism.'[195]

Heinz-Klaus Metzger was one of the first to take Adorno to task. 'Das Altern der Philosophie der neuen Musik', first broadcast on the WDR on 23 October 1957,[196] was later published with the designation 'Intermezzo I' in the fourth volume of *die*

---

[191] Goeyvaerts to Stockhausen, 24 September 1958; *Selbstlose Musik*, 386.

[192] The letter contains handwritten additions by Doris and Karlheinz; Doris writes 'What do you say? I'll answer'; Karlheinz writes 'Won't work! [*Geht nicht!*]' (ibid.). Goeyvaerts may well have anticipated a lack of response. For the first and only time in their correspondence, Goeyvaerts gives his last name in his signature, albeit parenthetically – 'Karel (Goeyvaerts)' – presumably in case the Stockhausens had forgotten him.

[193] Adorno, 'The Aging of New Music', in *Essays on Music*, ed. Richard Leppert, trans. Susan H. Gillespie (Berkeley: University of California Press, 2002), 192.

[194] Ibid.   [195] Ibid., 194.   [196] See Iddon, *New Music at Darmstadt*, 129.

Reihe in 1958, alongside an 'Intermezzo II' assembled by Eimert which – making the polemic argument that Adorno's criticism was little more than moribund neo-fascism from the Webern *Nachtprogramm* even more explicit – juxtaposes excerpts from 'Das Altern der neuen Musik' with 'remarks in a similar vein by one Hellmut Kotschenreuther' made at an unspecified earlier period of time; these remarks advance an unmistakably *Blut und Boden* ideology in their condemnation of modern music. Naturally, Metzger's contribution, translated idiomatically as 'Just Who Is Growing Old?',[197] is rather more nuanced: as with Eimert's gloss on Adorno's New Music and Adorno's gloss on Eimert's New Music, Metzger finds himself to be largely in agreement with his adversary – whom he describes as 'the first truly educated musician among philosophers' –[198] and, at most, simply accuses him of making a category mistake.[199] Indeed, Metzger asserts that Adorno's 'basic idea … of an objective historical tendency in musical material' in *Philosophie der neuen Musik* 'can scarcely be denied', and 'has been absorbed into the awareness of history which nowadays cannot be avoided by any young composer'.[200] Nevertheless, Adorno failed to follow through on his own model, leaving the Darmstadt School to pick up the slack: 'Following Webern, Metzger concluded, it was precisely Boulez, Stockhausen, and Pousseur … who had taken up the challenge to deal with the dialectic between these processes and compositional will. This was exactly what Adorno had suggested would be at the heart of a progressive compositional attitude to material.'[201]

However, in order to reconcile Adorno's discourse with the composers lumped together under the Darmstadt banner – in essence, presenting the Darmstadt School as what Adorno had been arguing for all along – Metzger is obliged to make a structural adjustment to the discursive formation of the Darmstadt School, one which involved the increasingly unreliable subject of Karel Goeyvaerts. Metzger hones in on the recourse to metaphysics which had

---

[197] While M. J. Grant is indeed correct to point out that the English translations of *die Reihe* were often awkward and haphazard affairs – and, indeed, the actual English text of 'Just Who Is Growing Old?' is far from elegant – the precise polemical formation of Metzger's argument is artfully maintained in translation. The ageing itself is not the issue, only the subject of the ageing; the model itself is not the issue, only the figures which populate it. Cf. M. J. Grant, *Serial Music, Serial Aesthetics: Compositional Theory in Post-War Europe* (Cambridge: Cambridge University Press, 2001).

[198] Heinz-Klaus Metzger, 'Just Who Is Growing Old?', trans. Leo Black, *die Reihe*, 4 (1960), 63.

[199] As Iddon remarks, 'Metzger's reproaches to Adorno are scathing, not in terms of his methodology but in the evidence he relies upon' (*New Music at Darmstadt*, 130). Metzger largely follows Eimert's characterisation of Adorno's category mistake as resulting, either consciously or not, in aesthetic neo-fascism, and gives the example of a particular critic who deployed Adorno's arguments to assert Werner Egk's *Die Zaubergeige* (1935), an extremely successful opera produced during the Third Reich which features the anti-Semitic 'Jude im Dorn' motif, as an example of an authentically progressive musical idiom. In fairness to all sides, of course, Egk had conducted his own works at Darmstadt.

[200] Metzger, 'Just Who Is Growing Old?', 63–4.   [201] Iddon, *New Music at Darmstadt*, 131.

so disturbed Adorno in this New Music, and, in a gesture of reassurance, isolates it as a uniquely unrepresentative discourse. To do so, he uses personal experience to equate it – not without reason – wholly with Karel Goeyvaerts and his music.

> If I remember rightly, in 1951 young Karel Goeyvaerts used this sort of argument when he brought his Opus 1 for two pianos to Adorno's composition class at Darmstadt. ... Again (and this I do recollect very clearly), Goeyvaerts used such 'exposition' in reply to Adorno's questions as to what his Opus 1 was 'about'. If it had ever occurred to Adorno to ask a composer like Boulez or Stockhausen about the 'function of some phenomenon within a work's total context of meaning' he would have been rudely awakened by a very different reply. Instead, he merely substituted the name Boulez for Goeyvaerts. It is clear from the essay ['Das Altern der Neuen Musik'] that one of its principal sources is this discussion with the young man from Antwerp, who is an artist of exemplary moral bearing and subjective attitude, but who seems, as regards the main point at issue, to have lost himself in deviation just as Hauer did in his time.[202]

Here Goeyvaerts, who was in fact one of the oldest of the Darmstadt composers, is relegated as 'the young man from Antwerp' to the barren, ex-centric subject position of New Music discourse. Just as Boulez had predicted, Goeyvaerts was neither an irrelevance nor an error, but fundamentally outside the proper dialectical unfolding of history: he was Hauer. To stabilise Metzger's ecumenical discourse of New Music and reassure Adorno that this music was exactly the self-critical, historically determined exposition of advanced musical material he had called for all along, Goeyvaerts is deployed – to use a metaphor the composer himself might have appreciated – as a Paschal lamb.

It is not surprising, then, that Adorno would react to Metzger's ecumenical criticism with an equally ecumenical gesture, 'entering into direct dialogue' with Metzger in a programme broadcast on the WDR on 19 February 1958.[203] Indeed, as Iddon notes, there was so little contention between the two theorists that the recording of this broadcast likely occurred in the summer of 1957 – well before Metzger had even publicly given his rebuttal.[204] The mutual 'concessions of ground' which Iddon chronicles over the course of this and subsequent exchanges, have, as Iddon confesses, a somewhat perfunctory character,[205] since Metzger had taken care to ensure that both theorists would be largely occupying the same territory from the outset. And of course, by this stage, Cage had already arrived on the scene,[206] making the exposition of post-Webernian methodology, whatever that may be, somewhat less of a pressing concern. The

---

[202] Metzger, 'Just Who Is Growing Old?', 79.   [203] Iddon, *New Music at Darmstadt*, 133.
[204] Ibid.   [205] Ibid., 133–41.   [206] See, generally, ibid., 167–228.

discourse of New Music now turned its attention to stabilising another, more aleatoric, set of practices.

In 1964, after Stockhausen had definitively abandoned *die Reihe*, Eimert published the first and only of a projected series of '*Bücher die Reihe*', titled *Foundations of Serial Technique in Music*.[207] The inventories and graphs are back in force, and the main body of the text is bifurcated by a table listing 1,928 of the 3,856 available all-interval series.[208] Eimert even finds space to compare Adorno to Spengler once again.[209] While such a settling of old scores and serial impulse for cataloguing, delineated in further chapters on possible spatial projections of intervallic material, might well seem out of touch with more recent musical production, Eimert's discourse is unmistakably directed at the newest of New Music. His teleology is still that of the *Atonale Musiklehre*: the autonomous, universal evolution of structural methods of musical organisation. By this date, Eimert expects the reader to be familiar with such an evolution and its attendant practice wherein 'musical elements are not only themselves ordered, but also connected to one another in ordered series of elements that creates a totality, a unity. This development process of integral composing', Eimert continues, 'is today not only straightforward but also recognizable in its limits.'[210] Predictably, these limits are overcome through technical progress, whereby 'the youngest music' has abandoned 'sterile seriality' to pursue 'aural, spatial, and interpretive actuation', a territory Eimert systematically charts for the bulk of his study.[211] Indeed, Eimert claims, remarkably, that the extraordinarily complex and rather fanciful geometrical functions he describes are exactly those which have already been adopted by leading composers.

> Compositional practice of rotation technique may be found with John Cage and his school, with Mauricio Kagel and Karlheinz Stockhausen. Cage's *Piano Concert* (1958) [*sic*] contains an abundance of rotation practices, of tone organisations in circular and curvilinear form through to obliquely situated line systems. Independently from Cage, Kagel has developed a systematic rotation technique in his works *Transicion I* (electronic, 1958) and *Transicion II* (1958/59) which allows groups of sounds to be rotated by

---

[207] Eimert, *Grundlagen der musikalischen Reihentechnik* (Vienna: Universal Edition, 1964).

[208] See ibid., 72–86. This inventory is so strikingly totalising that Toop uses it to illustrate 'the real death-blow to serialism . . . Suddenly, everything was there; you could no longer discover, only select'. See Richard Toop, 'Against a Theory of Musical (New) Complexity', in *Contemporary Music: Theoretical and Philosophical Perspectives*, ed. Max Paddison and Irène Deliège (Surrey: Ashgate, 2010), 97.

[209] Eimert, *Grundlagen*, 30.

[210] 'In solcher Zubereitung werden die musikalischen Elemente nicht nur in sich geordnet, sondern auch als geordnete Elementreihen so miteinander verbunden, daß sie ein Ganzes, eine Einheit bilden. Dieser Entwicklungsprozeß des integralen Komponierens ist heute nicht nur überschaubar, sondern auch in seinen Grenzen erkennbar.' Ibid., 10.

[211] Ibid., 11.

means of a turntable mounted on the score page and thus makes available the calculation of the rotational position through the angular function. Stockhausen employs rotation technique in his work *Refrain for three players* (1959), after he had already practiced composing with the circular form, representative in this context, in the piece named after it, *Zyklus*, 1959 (= circle).[212]

Thus, Eimert argues, these composers are merely following the ineluctable technical logic of twelve-tone technique into increasingly expanded conceptions of musical form.[213] By reading these composers as systematically following the course of technical progress inaugurated by Anton Webern,[214] Eimert presents a smooth continuity between the discursive formations of the Second Viennese School, serialism, and aleatoric and graphic music, not to mention the entirety of the Western art music tradition. Once again, the future was just like he imagined.

If Eimert's commentary here – his systematic, elaborate technical readings of works commonly understood to result from aleatoric processes or even less technical concerns – appears jarring, it is worth remembering that he is not arguing for anything particularly novel. Musical progress as autonomous refinement of technical processes had been Eimert's argument since the *Atonale Musiklehre* forty years earlier. Indeed, if the scientistic language is smoothed over and the context of an extraordinarily exhaustive manual for serial-geometrical transformations is put to one side, what Eimert presents is an eminently recognisable portrait of the 'second generation' of the Darmstadt School: John Cage, Mauricio Kagel, and, still, Karlheinz Stockhausen. Elsewhere, Eimert's reading of Cage is recognisably textbook, and even prefigures the emplotment of Helmut Lachenmann: Schoenberg's projected 'emancipation of dissonance', Eimert claims, was pursued logically by Cage into the 'emancipation of noise [*geräuschfarben*]'.[215] Eimert's reading may be ridiculous, but it is sensible.

---

[212] 'Kompositorische Anwendung von Rotationstechnik findet sich bei John Cage und seiner Schule, bei Mauricio Kagel und Karlheinz Stockhausen. Cages Klavierkonzert (1958) enthält eine Fülle von Rotationsanwendungen, von Tonanordnungen in Kreis- und Kurvenform bis zu schräg gestellten Liniensystemen. Unabhängig von Cage hat Kagel in seinen Werken "Transicion I" (elektronisch, 1958) und "Transicion II" (1958/59) eine konsequente Rotationstechnik entwickelt, die Tongruppen vermittels einer auf dem Notenblatt angebrachten Drehscheibe rotieren läßt und damit die Berechnung des Rotationsstandes durch die Winkelfunktion zugänglich gemacht hat. Stockhausen wendet Rotationstechnik in seinem Werk "Refrain für drei Spieler" (1959) an, nachdem er die in diesem Zusammenhang typische Kreisform bereits in dem danach benannten Stück "Zyklus", 1959 (= Kreis) kompositorisch praktiziert hatte.' Ibid., 132.

[213] Ibid., 132–3.

[214] Webern is still Eimert's touchstone figure; much of his graphic extrapolations of intervallic relations are illustrated through Webern's works, e.g. opp. 17, 20, 21, 23, 24, 25, 26, 27, 28, 29, 30, and 31. See ibid., 127–31.

[215] Ibid., 14.

And Eimert is not wrong, of course, there *are* circles in these works. There was independent treatment of musical parameters through 'synthetic number' in Goeyvaerts's Sonata as well. But Eimert's point once again is that not only are these composers using the *same* sort of circle (or 'systematic rotation technique', if you like), they are using it in pursuit of the same end, the expansion and refinement of technical procedures to organise sound material. In such a discourse, it is immaterial whether Cage has encountered the *I Ching* or Goeyvaerts is a practising Catholic: the curvilinear figures in the *Concert* are the same circles as those of any number of graphic scores; the number 7 is as good as any other. The only idea, the only phenomenon which may be found in New Music is the teleological course of technical mastery. Such a discourse is able to explain almost any musical practice, but it will always provide the same explanation. It is no wonder, then, that despite the almost overwhelming multiplicity of practices evident in both the concert programming and attendance of the Darmstädter Ferienkurse, historical accounts of New Music have only ever resulted in the same story.

5 Conclusion

While it would be simplistic to argue that Eimert functioned as a nearly monopolistic arbiter of New Music, it would not be inappropriate to attribute the role of theorist and cultural gatekeeper of a particular understanding of New Music – 'post-Webern', 'pointillist', and, above all, that of the 'Darmstadt School' – largely to Eimert. What is at stake here is not which music got performed and not even so much which composers were lionised, since, as a glance over the scheduled performances of any Darmstädter Ferienkurse during the first decade of its existence immediately reveals, the music under discussion here represents less than a fraction of a percentage of what was on display. On practical terms, then, it would be difficult to argue for an expanded place of authority for Eimert's writings, since the music he took as representative of the post-war avant-garde was almost never performed and, indeed, continues to be almost never performed. But it does continue to be taken as representative, to the exception of nearly all other musical activity. What is at stake, then, is an explicating discourse of New Music after World War II which has been maintained to this day.

Eric Salzman's *Twentieth-Century Music: An Introduction* was first published in 1967 by commercial textbook publisher Prentice Hall and has gone through four editions, the most recent of which was published in 2002.[216]

---

[216] Eric Salzman, *Twentieth-Century Music: An Introduction* (Upper Saddle River: Prentice Hall, 1967, fourth edition 2002).

Salzman distinguishes European New Music from its American counterpart (represented by Babbitt) by stating that, for European practitioners of serialism, '[t]he twelve-tone idea … is not a method (in Schoenberg's sense) nor a complex system (in Babbitt's sense) but rather a total generating principle through which a new and complete identity of materials, means, structure, and expression could be achieved'.[217] Thus, these composers charted 'all possible points of intersection' between different musical parameters in the course of composition. As an aside, Salzman notes: 'It is not quite accurate to say, as some commentators have, that this is music in which analysis precedes composition. The analysis is quite equivalent to the piece.'[218] The post-war generation are further described as 'Webernites' who 'did not hesitate to draw the most extreme conclusions' from the master's fixation on 'the individual, isolated sound event and the rational, organizing power of the serial principle'.[219] Stockhausen is the touchstone figure, 'the most influential architect and theorist of European Serialism'.[220] He is introduced in very nearly dictatorial terms:

> Stockhausen's initial concerns were the complete isolation and definition of every aspect of musical sound and the extension of serial control into every domain. The latter point is important: Stockhausen envisaged the possibility of serializing and thus pre-controlling even such matters as the density of harmonic, vertical masses; the number of musical events occurring in given time segments; the size of intervals and the choice of register; the types of attacks and articulations employed; the rate of change of texture and tone color.[221]

Salzman does point out that the 'reign' of European serialism was 'rather brief', but goes on to say that 'literally dozens and even hundreds of totally organized, post-Webern serial pieces were written, nearly all for small combinations of instruments and nearly all based on a highly rationalized arrangement of isolated, "pointillist" events and textures, often surrounded by generous amounts of highly organized silence'.[222] With an extremely liberal understanding of the categories of 'pointillism', 'post-Webern', and so on, there are ('literally') less than a dozen extant scores which might fit Salzman's description. These include Goeyvaerts's *Opus 2*, *Opus 3 met gestreken en geslagen tonen*, and *Nummer 6 met 180 klankvoorwerpen*; Stockhausen's *Kreuzspiel* and *Schlagtrio*; Michel Fano's *Étude pour 15 instruments*; and Herman Van San's *Sneden* and *Latticen*. Of these pieces, only Goeyvaerts's *Opus 2* and *Opus 3* and Stockhausen's *Kreuzspiel* had public performances in the early 1950s (Van San's *Sneden* was premiered as 'Opus 5' at the 1957 Ferienkurse). None of these scores were published in the 1950s; Fano's and

---

[217] Ibid., 160. [218] Ibid., 160, fn 1. [219] Ibid., 160. [220] Ibid., 161. [221] Ibid.
[222] Ibid., 160–1.

Van San's work remains unpublished. If Salzman's remark about 'highly organized silence' is taken at face value, Goeyvaerts's *Opus 3*, which uses rests as 'negative values' separating sounds, is in fact the *only* piece that fits such a description. Later, Salzman aligns this imaginary corpus with a 'positivist' conception of musical material, which (he claims) evolved into a 'structuralist' one in the later 1950s.[223]

It is very odd that a single piece by an obscure Flemish composer has come to represent the totality of avant-garde musical production in Europe in the early 1950s. But this was precisely the state of affairs that Eimert had described in his *Lehrbuch der Zwölftontechnik*. Of course, like Eimert and Adorno, these historians never let on that they are actually talking about Karel Goeyvaerts. Bryan R. Simm's *Music of the Twentieth Century: Style and Structure*, first published in 1986, follows Salzman in giving Stockhausen's *Kreuzspiel* as 'an example of post-war pointillism' which takes Webern as its sole model.[224] Subsequently, *Kreuzspiel* is later described as roughly equivalent to Boulez's *Structure Ia* '[i]n its rigorous application of serial procedures and elaborate pre-planning'.[225] Together, these practices represent the primary force shaping the European post-war avant-garde: the 'Darmstadt School', a group described, in an extremely telling conflation, as being 'founded in 1946'.[226]

It is clear that by this point Stockhausen and Boulez have become metonyms not only for the 'Darmstadt School' but the Darmstädter Ferienkurse in their entirety, even though, until the late 1950s, the courses themselves were largely devoted to Igor Stravinsky and Carl Orff. Of course, as everyone now knows, Orff is not New Music. Nor is the Stravinsky which was the subject of Strobel's discussion. But the Stravinsky who adopted an idiosyncratic method of organising hexachords is fitfully emplotted in the textbook narrative as a member of the old guard who strove 'to keep up with the times'.[227] These times are Eimert's times, where the international avant-garde boldly took up the telos of technical progress from where Webern had left it: 'At a memorial concert of his works at Darmstadt in 1953, Webern was hailed as the father of a new movement.'[228] In fact, this is the sole historical event mentioned in the section on 'Serialism' in Burkholder, Grout, and Palisca's textbook.

---

[223] Ibid., 185–6.

[224] Brian R. Simms, *Music of the Twentieth Century: Style and Structure* (New York: Schirmer, 1986).

[225] Ibid., 332.

[226] Ibid., 344–5. This error of dating speaks to the logic of this discourse – why *shouldn't* Stockhausen and Boulez have been there from the start? Why did 'zero hour' have to wait until 1951?

[227] Peter J. Burkholder, Donald J. Grout, and Claude V. Palisca, *A History of Western Music* (New York: Norton, 2006), 828.

[228] Ibid., 917.

What Eimert enacted was a discursive bait-and-switch. The technical processes used by (now, historically) marginal composers were used to explicate works by (now, historically) central composers. In the process, any other available reading of these musical practices was telescoped into Eimert's narrative of musical progress. Such a narrative has, by this late, post-everything date, come under vigorous criticism, most prominently by Georgina Born and Susan McClary.[229] Yet, like the textbooks, these critics take this narrative and its teleological claims at face value; their criticism does little to de-suture the music from the discourse. As such, their presentation of cultural hegemony misses the mark as soon as the claim is made that such a hegemony enjoyed any kind of stable, extra-discursive existence. In essence, they are still re-telling Eimert's story, aiming their critique at received categories rather than questioning how these categories came to be so seemingly enduring and self-evident in the first place. What is sorely needed now is a history of New Music which can devote itself to precisely that: the rich specificities of musical production.

---

[229] The most representative examples are Georgina Born, *Rationalizing Culture: IRCAM, Boulez, and the Institutionalization of the Musical Avant-Garde* (Berkeley: University of California Press, 1995) and Susan McClary, 'Terminal Prestige: The Case of Avant-Garde Music Composition', *Cultural Critique* 12 (1989), 57–81.

Bibliography

Adorno, Theodor W., 'Berg and Webern – Schönberg's Heirs', *Modern Music*, 8.2 (1931), 29–38

Essays on Music, ed. Richard Leppert (Berkeley: University of California Press, 2002)

Minima Moralia: Reflections from Damaged Life, trans. E. F. N. Jephcott (London: Verso, 1974)

'New Music and the Public: Some Problems of Interpretation', trans. Rollo H. Myers, in *Twentieth Century Music: A Symposium*, ed. Rollo H. Myers (London: John Calder, 1960), 40–51

Philosophie der neuen Musik, Gesammelte Schriften XII, ed. Rolf Tiedemann (Frankfurt am Main: Suhrkamp, 1975)

Quasi una Fantasia: Essays on Modern Music, trans. Rodney Livingstone (London: Verso, 1998)

'Spengler nach dem Untergang', *Der Monat*, 3.20 (1950), 115–28

Ashby, Arved, 'Of Modell-Typen and Reihenformen: Berg, Schoenberg, F. H. Klein and the Concept of Row Derivation', *Journal of the American Musicological Society*, 48 (1995), 67–105

Attali, Jacques, *Noise: The Political Economy of Music*, trans. Brian Massumi (Minneapolis: University of Minnesota Press, 1985)

Attinello, Paul, 'Postmodern or Modern: A Different Approach to Darmstadt', *Contemporary Music Review*, 26.1 (2007), 25–37

Blüggel, Christian, *E. = Ethik + Ästhetik: Zur Musikkritik Herbert Eimerts* (Saarbrücken: Pfau, 2002)

Blumröder, Christoph von, *Die Grundlegung der Musik Karlheinz Stockhausens* (Stuttgart: Franz Steiner, 1993)

'Orientation to Herman Hesse', trans. Jerome Kohl, *Perspectives of New Music*, 36.1 (1998), 65–96

Born, Georgina, *Rationalizing Culture: IRCAM, Boulez, and the Institutionalization of the Musical Avant-Garde* (Berkeley: University of California Press, 1995)

Burkholder, Peter J., Donald J. Grout, and Claude V. Palisca, *A History of Western Music* (New York: Norton, 2006)

Carroll, Mark, *Music and Ideology in Cold War Europe* (Cambridge: Cambridge University Press, 2003)

Chailley, Jacques, *La Musique Médiévale* (Paris: Du Courdrier, 1951)

Christiaens, Jan, '"Absolute Purity Projected into Sound": Goeyvaerts, Heidegger and Early Serialism', *Perspectives of New Music*, 41.1 (2003), 168–78

Chua, Daniel K. L., 'Drifting: The Dialectics of Adorno's Philosophy of New Music', in *Apparitions: New Perspectives on Adorno and Twentieth-Century Music*, ed. Berthold Hoeckner (Abingdon: Routledge, 2006), 1–18

Clark, Edward, 'The I. S. C. M. Festival', *The Musical Times*, 94.1326 (1953), 377–8

Claussen, Detlev, *Theodor W. Adorno: One Last Genius* (Cambridge: Harvard University Press, 2008)

Clifton, Thomas, *Music as Heard: A Study in Applied Phenomenology* (New Haven, CT: Yale University Press, 1983)

Collaer, Paul, *La Musique Moderne: 1905–1955* (Paris: Elsevier, 1955)

Dahlhaus, Carl, *Foundations of Music History*, trans. J. B. Robinson (Cambridge: Cambridge University Press, 1983)

Decroupet, Pascal, 'Développements et ramifications de la pensée sérielle. Recherches et oeuvres musicales de Pierre Boulez, Henri Pousseur et Karlheinz Stockhausen de 1951 à 1958'. Doctoral thesis, Université de Tours (1994)

Delaere, Mark, 'Auf der Suche nach serieller Stimmigkeit: Goeyvaerts' Weg zur Komposition Nr. 2 (1951)', *Die Anfänge der seriellen Musik*, ed. Orm Finnendahl (Berlin: wolke, 1999), 13–36

'"Jede kleine Leiche könnte ein Beethoven-Thema sein." Karel Goeyvaerts' Webern- Rezeption: Punkte und "tote Töne"', in *Anton Webern und das Komponieren im 20. Jahrhundert. Neue Perspektiven*, ed. Pietro Cavallotti and R. Schmusch (Vienna: Musikzeit, 2019), 231–48

'Olivier Messiaen's Analysis Seminar and the Development of Post-War Serial Music', trans. Richard Evans, *Music Analysis*, 21.1 (2002), 35–51

'The Projection in Time and Space of a Basic Idea Generating Structure: The Music of Karel Goeyvaerts', *Revue belge de Musicologie/Belgisch Tijdschrift voor Muziekweteschap*, 48 (1994), 11–14

'The Stockhausen-Goeyvaerts Correspondence and the Aesthetic Foundations of Serialism in the Early 1950s', in *The Musical Legacy of Karlheinz Stockhausen: Looking Back and Looking Forward*, ed. M. J. Grant and Imke Mische (Hofheim: wolke, 2016), 20–34

Delaere, Mark, ed., *Rewriting Recent Music History: The Development of Early Serialism 1947–1957* (Leuven: Peeters, 2011)

Delaere, Mark, Yves Knockaert, and Herman Sabbe, *Nieuwe muziek in Vlaanderen* (Bruges: Het Kunstboek, 1998)

Denmuth, Norman, *Musical Trends in the 20th Century* (London: Rockliff, 1952)

Desmet, Lieve, and Roel Vande Winkel, 'Historisch onderzoek naar de nieuwsproductie van de Vlaamse televisieomroep (NIR – BRT – BRTN – VRT):

Een praktijkgebaseerde bronnenanalyse', *Belgisch Tijdschrift voor Nieuwste Geschiedenis/Revue Belge d'Histoire Contemporaine*, 39 (2009), 93–122

Drew, David, 'The Darmstadt Summer School of New Music, 1954', *The Score and IMA Magazine*, 10 (December 1954), 77–81

Eggebrecht, Hans Heinrich, ed., *Terminologie der Musik im 20. Jahrhundert* (Stuttgart: Franz Steiner, 1995)

Eimert, Herbert, *Atonale Musiklehre* (Leipzig: Breitkopf & Härtel, 1924)

Grundlagen der musikalischen Reihentechnik (Vienna: Universal Edition, 1964)

Lehrbuch der Zwölftontechnik (Wiesbaden: Breitkopf & Härtel, 1952)

Ewen, David, *Modern Music: A History and Appreciation – from Wagner to the Avant-Garde* (Philadelphia: Chilton, 1962)

Feneyrou, Laurent, 'Entre l'écorce et le bourgeon: Trois analyses du Refrain de la "Danse Sacrale"', *Du politique en analyse musicale*, ed. Esteban Buch, Nicolas Donin, and Laurent Feneyrou (Paris: VRIN, 2013), 227–52

Fox, Christopher, 'Darmstadt and the Institutionalisation of Modernism', *Contemporary Music Review*, 26.1 (2007), 115–23

'Luigi Nono and the Darmstadt School: Form and Meaning in the Early Works (1950–1959)', *Luigi Nono: Fragments and Silence*, ed. Stephen Davismoon, *Contemporary Music Review*, 18.2 (1999), 111–30

'Other Darmstadts: An Introduction', *Contemporary Music Review*, 26.1 (2007), 1–3

Gallope, Michael, 'Why Was This Music Desirable? On a Critical Explanation of the Avant-Garde', *The Journal of Musicology*, 31.2 (2014), 199–230

Glock, William, ed. *Pierre Boulez: A Symposium* (London: Eulenburg, 1986)

Goeyvaerts, Karel, 'Paris – Darmstadt: 1947–1956: Excerpt from the Autobiographical Portrait', trans. Mark Delaere, *Revue belge de Musicologie/Belgisch Tijdschrift voor Muziekweteschap*, 48 (1994), 35–54

Selbstlose Musik: Texte • Briefe • Gespräche, ed. Mark Delaere (Cologne: MusikTexte, 2010)

Grant, M. J., *Serial Music, Serial Aesthetics: Compositional Theory in Post-War Europe* (Cambridge: Cambridge University Press, 2001)

Grant, M. J., and Imke Misch, eds., *The Musical Legacy of Karlheinz Stockhausen: Looking Back and Forward* (Hofheim: wolke, 2016)

Grassl, Markus, and Reinhard Kapp, eds., *Darmstadt-Gespräche* (Vienna: Böhlau, 1996)

Grier, James, *The Critical Editing of Music: History, Method, and Practice* (Cambridge: Cambridge University Press, 1996)

Griffiths, Paul, *The Sea on Fire: Jean Barraqué* (Rochester: University of Rochester Press, 2003)

Hall, Patricia, and Friedemann Sallis, eds, *A Handbook to Twentieth-Century Musical Sketches* (Cambridge: Cambridge University Press, 2004)

Harper-Scott, J. P. E., *The Quilting Points of Musical Modernism: Revolution, Reaction, and William Walton* (Cambridge: Cambridge University Press, 2012)

Harvey, Jonathan, *The Music of Stockhausen* (London: Faber & Faber, 1975)

Hauer, Josef Matthias, *Vom Melos zur Pauke: Eine Einführung in die Zwölftonmusik (Theoretische Schriften Band I)* (Vienna: Universal Edition, 1925)

Zwölftontechnik: Die Lehre von den Tropen (Theoretische Schriften Band II) (Vienna: Universal Edition, 1926)

Heile, Björn, 'Darmstadt as Other: British and American Responses to Musical Modernism', *Twentieth-Century Music*, 1.2 (2004), 161–78

Hodeir, André, 'Serialism and Developments in Western Music since Webern', trans. Rollo H. Myers, in *Twentieth Century Music: A Symposium*, ed. Rollo H. Myers (London: John Calder, 1960), 29–39

Since Debussy: A View of Contemporary Music (New York: Grove, 1961)

Iddon, Martin, 'Darmstadt Schools: Darmstadt as a Plural Phenomenon', *Tempo*, 65.256 (2011), 2–8

'Institutions, Artworlds, New Music', in *The Routledge Research Companion to Modernism in Music*, ed. Björn Heile and Charles Wilson (Abingdon: Routledge, 2019)

John Cage and David Tudor: Correspondence on Notation and Performance (Cambridge: Cambridge University Press, 2013)

New Music at Darmstadt: Nono, Stockhausen, Cage, and Boulez (Cambridge: Cambridge University Press, 2013)

'*Selbstlose Musik. Texte, Briefe, Gespräche* by Karel Goeyvaerts, Mark Delaere', review, *Notes*, 69.3 (2013), 531–5

'Serial Canon(s): Nono's *Variations* and Boulez's *Structures*', *Contemporary Music Review*, 29.3 (2010), 265–75

'Trying to Speak: Between Politics and Aesthetics, Darmstadt 1970–1972', *Twentieth- Century Music*, 3.2 (2007), 255–75

Iverson, Jennifer, *Electronic Inspirations: Technologies of the Cold War Musical Avant-Garde* (Oxford: University of Oxford Press, 2019)

Kirchmeyer, Helmut, *Kleine Monographie über Herbert Eimert* (Leipzig: Sächsischen Akademie der Wissenschaften, 1998)

'Stockhausens Elektronische Messe nebst einem Vorspann unveröffentlichter Briefe aus seiner Pariser Zeit an Herbert Eimert', *Archiv für Musikwissenschaft*, 66.3 (2009)

Kirchmeyer, Helmut, and Hugo Wolfram Schmidt, *Aufbruch der jungen Musik: Von Webern bis Stockhausen*, Die Garbe: Musikkunde Teil IV (Cologne: Hans Gerig, 1970)

Kovács, Inge, *Wege zum musikalischen Strukturalismus. René Leibowitz, Pierre Boulez, John Cage und die Webern-Rezeption in Paris um 1950* (Schliengen: Argus, 2004)

Kurtz, Michael, *Stockhausen: A Biography*, trans. Richard Toop (London: Faber & Faber, 1992)

Machlis, Joseph, *Introduction to Contemporary Music* (London: Dent, 1961)

Maconie, Robin, *The Works of Karlheinz Stockhausen* (London: Oxford University Press, 1976)

   The Works of Karlheinz Stockhausen, 2nd ed. (London: Oxford University Press, 1990)

Marie, Jean-Étienne, *Musique Vivante: introduction au langage musical contemporain* (Paris: Privat, 1953)

Marino, Stefano, 'La ricezione dell'estetica musicale di Th.W Adorno in Italia' (unpublished PhD thesis, University of Bologna, 2001)

McClary, Susan, 'Terminal Prestige: The Case of Avant-Garde Music Composition', *Cultural Critique* 12 (1989), 57–81.

Messiaen, Olivier, *The Technique of My Musical Language*, trans. John Satterfield (Paris: Alphonse Leduc, 1956)

Metzger, Heinz-Klaus, 'Just Who Is Growing Old?', trans. Leo Black, *die Reihe*, 4 (1960), 63–80

Metzger, Heinz-Klaus, and Rainer Riehn, eds., *Karlheinz Stockhausen: ... wie die Zeit verging ..., Musik-Konzepte*, 19 (Munich: text + kritik, 1981)

Misch, Inge, and Markus Brandur, eds., *Karlheinz Stockhausen bei den Internationalen Ferienkursen für Neue Musik Darmstadt 1951–1996: Dokumente und Briefe* (Kürten: Stockhausen, 2001)

Morgan, Robert P., *Twentieth-Century Music: A History of Musical Style in Modern Europe and America* (New York: Norton, 1991)

Nielinger-Vakil, Carola, *Luigi Nono: A Composer in Context* (Cambridge: Cambridge University Press, 2015)

Pace, Ian, 'The Reconstruction of Post-War West German New Music during the early Allied Occupation (1945–46), and Its Roots in the Weimar Republic and Third Reich (1918–45)' (unpublished PhD thesis, University of Cardiff, 2018)

Paddison, Max, *Adorno's Aesthetics of Music* (Cambridge: Cambridge University Press, 1993)

Peyser, Joan, *Boulez: Conductor, Composer, Enigma* (London: Cassell, 1976)

Piccardi, Carlo, 'Tra ragioni umane e ragioni estetiche: i dodecafonici a congresso', in *Norme con Ironie: scritti per i settant'anni di Ennio Morricone*, ed. Laura Gallenga (Milan: Suivini Zerboni, 1998), 205–72

Piekut, Benjamin, *Experimentalism Otherwise: The New York Avant-Garde and Its Limits* (Berkeley: University of California Press, 2011)

Prieberg, Fred K., *Handbuch Deutsche Musiker 1933–1945* (Auprès de Zombry: Fred K. Prieberg, 2004)

Ross, Alex, *The Rest Is Noise: Listening to the Twentieth Century* (London: Harper Perennial, 2007)

Sabbe, Herman, 'Comentaar', in *Documenta Musicae Novae I*, Publikaties van het seminarie voor muziekgeschiedenis, 3 (Ghent: Rijksuniversiteit-Gent, 1968), unpaginated

'Die Einheit der Stockhausen-Zeit: Neue Erkenntnismöglichkeit der seriellen Entwicklung anhand des frühen Wirkens von Stockhausen und Goeyvaerts. Dargestellt aufgrund der Briefe Stockhausens an Goeyvaerts', *Karlheinz Stockhausen: ... wie die Zeit verging ...*, *Musik-Konzepte*, vol. 19 (Munich: text + kritik, 1981), 5–96

'Das Musikdenken von Karel Goeyvaerts in Bezug auf das Schaffen von Karlheinz Stockhausen: Ein Beitrag zur Geschichte der frühseriellen und elektronischen Musik 1950–1956', *Interface. Journal of New Music Research*, 2.1 (1973), 101–13

'Goeyvaerts and the Beginnings of "Punctual" Serialism and Electronic Music', *Revue belge de Musicologie/Belgisch Tijdschrift voor Muziekweteschap*, 48 (1994), 55–94

Het muzikale serialisme als techniek en als denkmethode (Ghent: Rijksuniversiteit-Gent, 1977)

'The New Music in the 20th Century – A Number of Key Concepts Essential For Interpretation', in *Inter Disciplinas Ars*, ed. Peter Dejans (Leuven: Leuven University Press, 1998), 81–92

'A Paradigm of "Absolute Music": Goeyvaerts's No. 4 as "Numerus Sonorus"', *Revue belge de Musicologie/Belgisch Tijdschrift voor Muziekweteschap*, 59 (2005), 243–51

'Techniques médiévales en musique contemporaine: histoire de la musique et sens culturel', *Revue belge de Musicologie/Belgisch Tijdschrift voor Muziekweteschap*, 34/35 (1980/1981), 220–33

Salzman, Eric, *Twentieth-Century Music: An Introduction* (Upper Saddle River: Prentice Hall, 1967, fourth edition 2002)

Saunders, Frances Stonor, *Who Paid the Piper?: The CIA and the Cultural Cold War* (London: Granta, 1999)

Schiffer, Brigitte, 'The Citadel of the Avant-Garde', *World of Music*, 11.3 (1969), 32–43

Schneider, Urs Peter, *Konzeptuelle Musik: Eine kommentierte Anthologie* (Bern: Aart Verlag, 2016)

Simms, Brian R., *Music of the Twentieth Century: Style and Structure* (New York: Schirmer, 1986)

Slonimsky, Nicolas, *Music Since 1900* (New York: Schirmer, 1937, fifth edition 1994)

Smith Brindle, Reginald, *The New Music: The Avant-Garde Since 1945* (London: Oxford University Press, 1975)

Steinecke, Wolfgang, 'Kranichstein – Geschichte, Idee, Ergebnisse', *Darmstädter Beiträge zur neuen Musik*, 4 (1962), 9–24

Stephan, Rudolf, Lothar Knessl, Otto Tomek, Klaus Trapp, and Christopher Fox, eds., *Von Kranichstein zur Gegenwart* (Stuttgart: DACO, 1996)

Stockhausen, Karlheinz, *Texte zur Musik, 1970–1977*, vol. 4 (Cologne: DuMont, 1978)

　　Towards a Cosmic Music, trans. Tim Nevill (Longmead: Element, 1989)

　　'Weberns Konzert für 9 Instrumente op. 24: Analyse des ersten Satzes', *Melos*, 20.12 (1953), 343–8

Stuckenschmidt, Hans Heinz, *Twentieth-Century Composers, Volume II: Germany and Central Europe*, ed. Anna Kallin and Nicolas Nabokov (London: Weidenfeld and Nicolson, 1970)

Taruskin, Richard, *Music in the Late Twentieth Century, The Oxford History of Western Music*, vol. V (Oxford: Oxford University Press, 2005)

Toop, Richard, 'Against a Theory of Musical (New) Complexity', *Contemporary Music: Theoretical and Philosophical Perspectives*, ed. Max Paddison and Irène Deliège (Surrey: Ashgate, 2010), 89–98

　　'Messiaen/Goeyvaerts, Fano/Stockhausen, Boulez', *Perspectives of New Music*, 13.1 (1974), 141–69

Trudu, Antonio, *La "Scuola" di Darmstadt: I Ferienkurse dal 1946 a oggi* (Milan: Edizioni Unicopoli, 1992)

Ungeheuer, Elena, *Wie die elektronische Musik 'erfunden' wurde … : Quellenstudie zu Werner Meyer-Epplers Entwurf zwischen 1949 und 1953* (Mainz: Schott, 1992)

Weaver, Jennifer L., 'Theorizing Atonality: Herbert Eimert's and Jefim Golyscheff's Contributions to Composing with Twelve Tones' (unpublished PhD thesis, University of North Texas, 2014)

Webern, Anton, *Letters to Hildegard Jone and Josef Humplik*, ed. Josef Polnauer, trans. Cornelius Cardew (Bryn Mawr, PA: Theodore Presser, 1967)

The Path to the New Music, ed. Willi Reich, trans. Leo Black (Bryn Mawr, PA: Theodore Presser, 1963)

Whittall, Arnold, *Serialism* (Cambridge: Cambridge University Press, 2008)

Williams, Alistair, *New Music and the Claims of Modernity* (Aldershot: Ashgate, 1997)

'New Music, Late Style: Adorno's "Form in the New Music"', *Music Analysis*, 27.2–3 (2008), 193–9

Wörner, Karl H., *Stockhausen: Life and Work*, trans. Bill Hopkins (Berkeley: University of California Press, 1973)

Cambridge Elements ≡

Music Since 1945

Mervyn Cooke
University of Nottingham

Mervyn Cooke brings to the role of series editor an unusually broad range of expertise, having published widely in the fields of twentieth-century opera, concert and theatre music, jazz, and film music. He has edited and co-edited *Cambridge Companions to Britten, Jazz, Twentieth-Century Opera*, and *Film Music*. His other books include *Britten: War Requiem, Britten and the Far East, A History of Film Music, The Hollywood Film Music Reader, Pat Metheny: The ECM Years*, and two illustrated histories of jazz. He is currently co-editing (with Christopher R. Wilson) *The Oxford Handbook of Shakespeare and Music*.

About the Series

Elements in Music Since 1945 is a highly stimulating collection of authoritative online essays that reflects the latest research into a wide range of musical topics of international significance since the Second World War. Individual Elements are organised into constantly evolving clusters devoted to such topics as art music, jazz, music and image, stage and screen genres, music and media, music and place, immersive music, music and movement, music and politics, music and conflict, and music and society. The latest research questions in theory, criticism, musicology, composition and performance are also given cutting-edge and thought-provoking coverage. The digital-first format allows authors to respond rapidly to new research trends, with contributions being updated to reflect the latest thinking in their fields, and the essays are enhanced by the provision of an exciting range of online resources.

Cambridge Elements ≡

Music Since 1945

Printed in the United States
By Bookmasters